BASIC **W**OODTURNING **T**ECHNIQUES

David Regester

BETTERWAY BOOKS · CINCINNATI, OHIO

First published 1993

© David Regester, 1993

First published in the U.S.A. by Betterway
Books, an imprint of F&W Publications, Inc.,
1507 Dana Avenue, Cincinnati, Ohio 45207

Typeset by Servis Filmsetting Ltd,
Manchester
and printed in Great Britain
by The Bath Press, Avon

Published by
B.T. Batsford Ltd
4 Fitzhardinge Street
London W1H 0AH

ISBN 1 55870 300 4

CONTENTS

INTRODUCTION

My qualifications for writing this book do not consist of formal training, since none is available in Great Britain or the United States, but through the practical experience I have gained by working full-time at my trade since 1974. During this time I have worked out some effective ways of making the relatively large number of items that constitute my stock-in-trade.

Woodturning was not my first choice of profession and I tried being an articled clerk in a solicitor's office and then a student of English and Philosophy before deciding that my talents lay in my hands rather than my brain. I started my turning as a hobby using a lathe attachment to an electric drill, a small selection of tools and a book that purported to tell you how it was done. All three had severe limitations, but I had sufficient success to encourage me to think that I might eventually become fairly proficient.

I could not afford any training so I found a free workshop at a craft centre in Devon and continued to teach myself while under the public gaze. When

Richard Raffan saw the pieces I had submitted to the Devon Guild of Craftsmen, in my first unsuccessful application for full membership, he generously allowed me to attend his workshop in Topsham (Devon) where I was able to watch a woodturner at work for the first time. It is remarkable how quickly you can learn after struggling on your own and making mistakes.

That was in 1975 when public demonstrations of turning were much rarer in England than they are today. The move towards a more sharing attitude to turning skills started in the United States where it brought about the inauguration in 1985 of the American Association of Woodturners (see Useful Addresses p. 108). Great Britain followed in 1987, largely due to the efforts of Ray Key, and the Association of Woodturners of Great Britain (see Useful Addresses p. 108) was formed. There are now national associations in many countries and all have national and local meetings where demonstrations are a feature.

My first piece of advice is to join your national association and contact your local branch, where you can meet fellow turners of every level of ability and have the opportunity to watch a wide range of turning demonstrated. Many professional turners now realise that it is only by helping each other that we raise the general level of skill in our craft. In turn, this should lead to exponents being able to concentrate more on design, so raising the quality of turning available to the public and enhancing their opinion of our craft.

Because I started my career at a craft centre I was expected to supply the shop with a range of items that sold, and for someone trying to earn a living this is a good discipline. Eventually, I formulated a range of designs for domestic items and could repeat them to order. I now supply high-class kitchenware shops with this type of work, and galleries and exhibitions with one-off pieces.

To my mind a good woodturner is one who makes well-designed and well-finished goods that people want to possess and use and, in the case of a professional, that he produces efficiently enough for them to be able to afford and for him to live on the proceeds. Committees and intellectuals decide if what you produce is Art; people decide if what you produce is desirable. Both can be fickle masters so you had best make up your own mind about what you want to aim for and then go for it.

As a professional woodturner, I have made a point of not concentrating on a limited range because I feel that as a result I am a more complete turner. No doubt it is more efficient to make just one sort of object, but I would find it rather boring. If you agree with me, and try to learn a full repertoire of techniques, you will find that you are able to make most things that you can imagine

or that others have made before you.

Woodturning is a creative and rewarding hobby that I would like more people to become more proficient in. In my experience, it is similar to most other arts and crafts in that you must practise the basic skills before you can create a masterpiece. I have tried to design this book to facilitate this process by organizing the information in easy-to-distinguish sections that can be used in different ways. **Part One** consists of chapters of general information that should be read before you lay out any money on equipment or materials. **Part Two** consists of chapters on technique, intended to be practised as a pianist would do scales.

Throughout the book I explain the methods that work for me. However, they should be

regarded as just the starting point for your exploration of woodturning and while it is a mistake to think that there is only one way of doing anything, following one method that definitely works does give you a firm base to start from. You can soon tell if the new method is really better than the old and your mistakes will hopefully be less painful.

Remember that you learn more from mistakes than successes and that if you are an occasional turner you are likely to forget your bloomers from one session to the next. Why not keep a record of your blunders in a notebook to remind you? You will probably be able to remember your successes without recording them!

PART ONE

TOOLS, EQUIPMENT AND MATERIALS

THE LATHE

A lathe is simply a machine for rotating a piece of wood so that a tool can be held against the wood for the purpose of altering its shape. Many turners, like myself, have started their turning with a lathe attachment to an electric drill. This is all well and dandy, to see if you like turning, but as soon as you want to turn anything larger than the average toothpick you will burn out your drill or wear out its bearings.

This suggests the first point that you must decide when selecting a lathe, namely, what do you want to turn? However, you do not know what you want to turn until you start turning, and you cannot do this until you have access to a lathe.

Whenever you intend to invest in something as expensive as a lathe it makes sense to talk to as many people as possible about their experiences. When you have joined your local turning group you will be able to find out who has what, and if you play your cards right you might be allowed to see the beasts in question. I do not recommend asking your local professional, for, unless he sells lathes, you

will be cutting into his production time and unless you compensate him for this he will probably not be all that helpful.

Visit exhibitions of turning to see what you like, and do a course to see what you have an aptitude for. If you decide that you only want to turn lace bobbins then you can do all you want to do on a small lathe, but the chances are that once you get started you will want to turn bigger things. The first rule of buying machinery states that you will always need a larger machine than the one you have just bought. Therefore, the answer to which lathe to buy would seem to be: as big as you can afford and can fit into your workshop. You can save money by buying a second-hand lathe if you can find the right one at the right price, but you could be buying someone else's problem if you do not know what you are looking for. A good compromise here is to buy a reconditioned lathe from one of the firms specializing in the field.

The size of a lathe is described in terms of first, the distance between centres (the maximum

length you can turn) and second, its swing, which is the largest diameter of disc you can turn. This last figure is double the height of the centre from the bed.

Here is a check list of points which I suggest you pay particular attention to when looking for a lathe (**fig. 1**).

MOTOR

For occasional use, or on a lathe with, say, a 20cm (8in) swing, a motor of 250 to 375 watts ($\frac{1}{3}$ to $\frac{1}{2}$hp) should be sufficient. If you intend to make anything larger, or do it on a more regular basis, you will need at least 750 watts (1hp). Do not rely simply on the manufacturer's rating as it is the thickness of the wire and the number of coils in the windings that affect the power. This is usually reflected in the price, so that an expensive motor may well be more powerful than a cheaper one of the same rating. A three phase motor is usually more powerful than its single phase equivalent, particularly when it has a lower rpm.

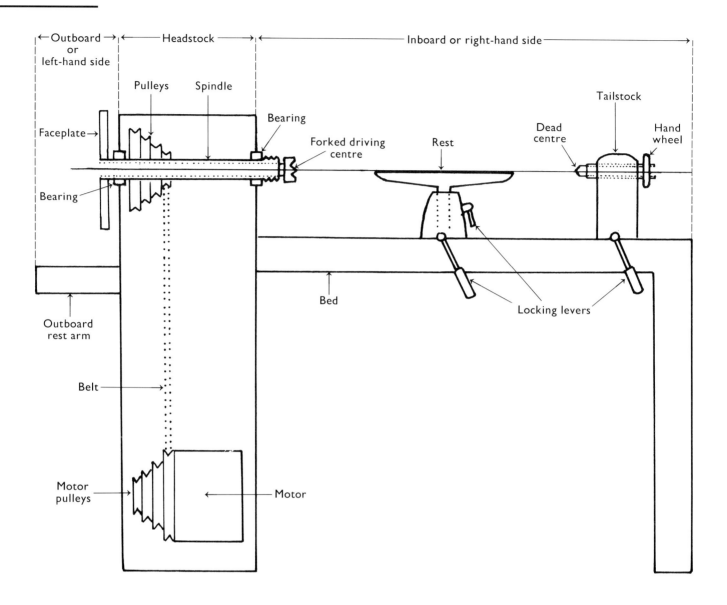

Fig. 1
Lathe

If you can find a good second-hand lathe it may well be better than a new one because the old motors tend to be better made. You may need it to be renovated by one of the firms specializing in this work, but it will be worth it.

There is no point in having a motor bigger than 1500 watts (2hp) for normal use because the amount of electricity it uses becomes very expensive. Though three phase power is not a domestic supply, if you do have it on site then go without hesitation for a three phase motor. It is usually prohibitively expensive to convert your supply to three phase but there are conversion units on the market that make it feasible to run a three phase motor off single phase power, particularly if you have been able to pick up a good second-hand lathe cheaply.

BEARINGS

Bearings should be as big and as heavy as possible. They have to take the sideways thrust when working between centres and stand up to all the forces exerted when an eccentric bowl blank is wobbling away on the faceplate. Go for sealed-for-life ones if possible because you do not have to worry about whether you are lubricating them correctly; it is bad to over-grease ordinary bearings because this slows them down and grease tends to work out of the housing and make a mess. With all bearings listen for excessive noise as this tells you how good they are, how well-fitted and whether you can stand listening to them all day. Tapered bearings are fitted to at least one make of lathe and these can be adjusted to take account of wear. You may well find that by the time you need to do this they will be so worn that you would do better to replace them. The bearings are located in the headstock, which again needs to be as massive as possible to support them.

SPINDLE

This should be at least 37.5mm (1½in) in diameter and have a hole through the middle so that you can pass a bar through it to release the driving centre. It should be tapered to take the centre and this will be described as morse number two or three, which is just a standard way of describing the taper – the larger the number, the bigger the hole. For a 37.5mm spindle this should be three.

SPEEDS

The motor shaft rotates at one speed all the time, but the rotational speed required for the wood varies with its size, its concentricity or otherwise, its coarseness of grain and the skill of the user. The most simple and, therefore, most foolproof way of changing the speed is for there to be four different-sized pulleys on the motor and four more on the spindle with a belt to transfer the power from the motor.

There are some problems with this method. First, it takes time and some effort to change the belt over from one pulley to the other, and second, there are times when the speed required is between two of the steps. This occurs when the blank is too big for one speed but too small for the next speed, so that you turn it too slowly for efficiency or too quickly for safety.

A range of speeds of 425, 790, 1330 and 2250 rpm should prove adequate unless you wish to turn bowls larger than 50cm (19½in), in which case speeds as low as 50 rpm could be useful.

Sometimes the blank is eccentric due either to being cut inaccurately or as a result of differences of density within the wood. It often happens that the one speed at which the wood will rotate without wobbling is between the steps.

The answer to these problems lies in some form of variable speed. More lathes are now being fitted with variable speed as standard and this is done, either

by mechanical means, electronically, or a combination of both. Check any lathe fitted with electronic speed control for loss of torque (rotary force) at both extremes of speed. If the full range of speeds is provided electronically, it usually means that there has been a compromise on torque at one end of the spectrum.

There are also kits on the market which convert your lathe to variable speed. These give electronic speed variation while retaining three pulleys. You have a range of speeds between 250 to 900 rpm on the smallest motor pulley and 600 to 2200 rpm on the largest. This solves the torque problem because the electronics do not have to provide the full range of speeds. Select the range of speeds you are likely to need before you start, select the correct pulley, and all the adjustments you need to do after that are by means of the switch.

CONSTRUCTION

Again the best lathes are the most sturdily constructed. A cast-iron body (see Useful Addresses for suppliers) absorbs vibrations and helps to prevent the lathe wandering around the workshop if you have an eccentric blank on board and have not bolted the lathe to the floor.

The cheapest lathes are made without stands and are intended to be bolted to a homemade stand. If you have one of these then you really have to make the stand out of heavy members (wood or metal) and add to the weight of the whole construction, perhaps by filling the base with sand. Turning is difficult enough without having to cope with the lathe vibrating.

Mid-price lathes often have stands which are made of sheet metal or box girders. These look stable enough, but if you try to turn a large, wet, eccentric blank of oak on them, they soon go walkies. This can again be solved by attaching sheets of strong board or metal to the members and filling with sand.

TOOL REST

Your tool is supported by this at all times and it needs to be both firm and easily movable. It is a straight piece of metal, supported at right angles by a shaft which needs to be at least 25mm (1in) in diameter for the larger lathe. It should be made of metal that is softer than the tool and can be filed to restore its smooth surface when it is scored by that inevitable catch. I prefer its upper edge to be rounded so that the tool can be moved over its surface in all planes in a flowing motion (see fig. 50, p. 61).

The rest is supported by an arm that slides along the bed and is locked in place when the rest is in its correct position. Better lathes have a lever which locks the rest support in place. Avoid those lathes which require spanners to do this as they are just too awkward.

TAILSTOCK

When turning between centres, the end of the work not in contact with the driving centre is supported by a pointed piece of metal. In some cases this is fixed and allows the wood to rotate because of lubrication, in the form of wax, applied to the point of contact on the end of the wood. This point of metal is called the dead centre and it invariably gets hot and burns into the end of the work, not the least disadvantage of which is the constant necessity to take up the slack this causes. Also, it is not as satisfactory as a rotating centre which does not offer any resistance to the wood. Even if your lathe manufacturer does not supply a rotating centre there should be a hole through the tailstock with a morse taper that will enable you to fit one. If you intend to make lampstands you will need a tailstock with a hole all the way through it for drilling the hole for the lead.

The tailstock will move along the bed, and, as with the rest, the support should be lockable by lever. Fine adjustment is carried out by the dead centre being held in a threaded shaft (often called the tailstock barrel) which moves in and out, preferably by means of a hand wheel. The position of the dead centre is then

maintained by a locking screw. On my lathe this is a small knurled knob which I found difficult to tighten until I modified it by drilling a hole through it, to take a lever which in its previous life had masqueraded as a 10cm (4in) nail.

It is very important that the dead centre is perfectly in line with an imaginary line drawn through the centre of the spindle. If this is not the case, centre work will vibrate when turning and in extreme cases it can be almost impossible to finish. You may be able to obtain a jig to test this but a rough and ready check (which will suffice for most uses) is to support as long a spindle as you can fit between centres by holding it in a four jaw chuck. If all is well and you rotate it slowly while bringing up the dead centre, the dead centre should make one mark in the centre. If the dead centre is not correctly aligned, it will mark a circle in the end. It may be possible to adjust the bed so that the dead centre is correctly aligned by putting metal shims between the bed and the body of the lathe.

DRIVING CENTRE

This is the part that fits in the shaft and causes the wood to rotate. It is made with either two flats or four (or even with spitzes) and can also be obtained in different sizes to cater for different diameters of wood.

They consist of fairly soft metal so you can easily modify their shape if required. The flats have sharp edges and must be kept in that condition if they are to be efficient.

BOWL TURNING CAPACITY

In order to cater for turning bowls of a larger diameter than the swing over the bed, lathe manufacturers have come up with a variety of ploys. The simplest of these is to fit on the outboard side of the lathe a rest arm lower than the bed on the inboard side. This allows you to turn a larger diameter bowl on the outboard side than over the bed, and also provides access all around the bowl which is not possible over the bed.

Another solution is to have the motor and headstock in a unit fitted on the bed. This is then rotated through 90° or 180° which enables the bowl to project beyond the body of the lathe. The rest is supported either on an extension from the rest arm on the bed, which is not really strong enough, or on a floor rest, which is the best option, because the size of bowl is then limited only by the height of the lathe from the floor. The rotating headstock unit is not a serious option for the more committed bowl turner because it has to be movable, which means that it will not be totally rigid. It is generally held in place by screws, and

screws on a vibrating lathe always work loose. The fact that the motor and the pulleys are all housed in a unit which fits above the bed also means that they are not robust or powerful enough for someone who intends turning many large bowls.

Some lathes have a gap in the bed at the headstock end to allow for larger diameter work at this point. This is all right if the combined bowl and chuck depth is not too deep to fit in the gap, and you do not mind working over the bed.

The best lathe for bowl turning that I have used has an outboard rest arm for bowls up to 50cm (19½in) in diameter, allied with a short bed with no supporting legs which allows for the same swing over the bed. I turn all my bowls on this side because the extra grooves in the bed give you more positions for the rest. You can even remove the bed and support the rest on a free-standing support for bowls larger than 50cm diameter. This lathe is even better with variable speed and needs a larger motor than the standard 550 watts if you do intend making large bowls.

One of the oldest types of lathe and the one from which the name may well have been derived is the pole lathe, as used by the bodgers in the woods around High Wycombe. These itinerant turners specialized in turning legs and other parts of Windsor chairs and worked in the woods where their timber grew. They constructed their lathes on the spot using a sapling and treadle

to impart a reciprocating motion on the work they were turning. If you wish to emulate them, you will become the greenest of green turners and I wish you luck. Plans of a pole lathe may be obtained from High Wycombe Museum, England and you even have a specialized Association to join (see address on p. 108).

Whatever lathe you eventually select it will generally need to be raised so that you can work on it without bending. I find that a comfortable height for me is where my elbows are level with the driving centre when I am standing upright. It is far better for the lathe to be too high so that you reach up than for it to be too low so that you have to bend down.

I have raised my lathe by having the local blacksmith weld together three short lengths of steel girder into a triangle. Some lathes have several holes in the base which enable you to screw them to a stand, and the stand, being made of girders, has flanges round the edge which can be screwed into the floor. If you should find that the lathe is too high it is easy to construct a platform on which to stand.

Since the perfect lathe does not exist, the one you eventually buy will inevitably be a compromise. You should not be afraid to modify it to make it closer to perfection.

—2—

THE WORKSHOP

Not many people have the opportunity or the means to do their turning in a purpose-built workshop. Most of us have to make do with a garage or a shed at the bottom of the garden and we generally have to share the accommodation, perhaps with a car and a wide variety of other miscellaneous equipment. I shall assume that you have room for everything you need and the money to pay for it, but if you have not, I hope to supply you with enough information to make the best compromises. **Fig. 2** is an idealized plan of my workshop.

Safety is paramount. In the workshop you are going to use electricity which can kill and machinery which can both injure if misused, and produce dust, which can damage your health in the long term. Good planning before you start can reduce these risks, but in the end, however well you have organized yourself, it takes only a moment's carelessness to do yourself an injury.

ELECTRICITY

Electricity can kill in an instant

and faulty wiring can cause fire, so I strongly recommend that you have any electrical work done by a qualified electrician. Tell him what machinery you intend to use and ask for a circuit breaker to be installed so that if you do cut into the wiring the supply will be cut off instantly.

Work out how many sockets you are going to need and add several where you do not think you will need them so that when you change things around to accommodate that new bit of machinery you will not have to get the electrician to call again. If you can install sockets on the ceiling you will find them invaluable for avoiding trailing leads, which are very dangerous.

LIGHTING AND HEATING

Natural lighting is the best, so have as many windows as you can. If these are in the ceiling or facing south in the northern hemisphere they will need shading when the sun is strong, but it is a small price to pay for good light. Windows that open

are excellent forms of ventilation when the weather outside is good, though this will mean additional arrangements for dust extraction.

If and when natural lighting is not available you will need some artificial light. Fluorescent tubes are fine for background lighting but are not recommended for work close to the lathe as they produce quite the wrong sort of light. You need two light sources close to the lathe. I have a dentist's light over the lathe and an angle poise to the side for shining into, and sometimes through, bowls.

For most people some kind of artificial heat source is needed at some time. In the presence of combustible materials you must avoid heat sources that can ignite flying wood shavings. This rules out gas fires with exposed flames and electric fires where the elements could contact the material, such as some convector heaters. Expert advice on this subject can be sought from your local fire safety officer and, perhaps, a retailer of heaters. In any event, a smoke alarm (ideally connected to the house) would

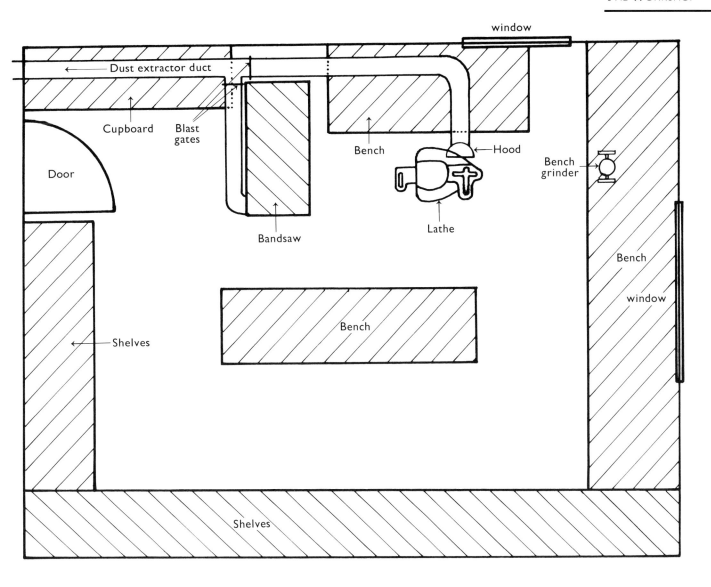

window

Dust extractor duct

Cupboard   Blast
gates

Door

Bench

Hood

Bench
grinder

Lathe

Bandsaw

Bench

Bench

window

Shelves

Bench

Shelves

Fig. 2
Workshop

give timely warning should a fire occur and a fire extinguisher (regularly checked) can put out a fire before it spreads.

Whatever heat source you select, it pays, and is environmentally sensible, to insulate your workshop. This will also reduce the amount of noise to which you expose your

neighbours. The type of insulation you install will depend on the construction of the building but I would strongly suggest that you do not forget the floor. Not only is a lot of heat lost through the floor but it is hard on the feet and legs to stand for a long period on a cold floor.

The ideal flooring in my experience is a layer of concrete (so that you can bolt any machinery to the floor) topped by a layer of flooring-grade expanded polystyrene with

flooring-grade particle board on top of that. Not only does that keep your feet warm, but it is easier on the joints than concrete. Two other advantages of this floating floor are that if you drop a tool, it will not be damaged, and also, it absorbs vibrations from machinery rather than reflecting the vibrations back into the machine. You may still need to bolt your machinery to the floor but this can be done through the floating floor with expanding bolts.

FIRST AID

It is sensible to give some thought to what will happen if all your caution comes to nought and you suffer some injury. In the worst case you could be rendered unconscious, so, strictly speaking, it is not wise to work on your own, or at least where you will not be missed if you do not surface for a few hours. A phone in the workshop could enable you to summon assistance should a less serious injury happen, but do think before the event what number to ring and make a note of it by the phone.

A first aid kit is essential for cuts and grazes, and should be kept in a dust-free but easy-to-open container. I also have an aerosol can of spray to hand at all times for reducing the immediate swelling and pain of a bruising injury.

DUST EXTRACTION

Dust is a peril in several ways; it can be a fire hazard if there are naked flames and, in extreme cases, spontaneous combustion can occur. Any dust can cause immediate breathing difficulties or irritation to sensitive parts such as eyes; and some people are allergic to certain dusts. Dust from some woods is even poisonous. This is commoner in timbers from tropical areas, where they have developed toxins as defences against the many insects that regard them as

food, than in woods from temperate climes.

These dangers take immediate effect, but the worst hazard is the permanent damage that can occur as a result of long-term exposure to even low levels of non-toxic dust. By the time you notice that that cough is not going away it is too late. There was a well-documented spate of nasal cancers in High Wycombe, England, among woodworkers in the furniture trade. This was associated with exposure to wood dust, and although this illness is rare, it is advisable to be aware of the possibility and to take precautions to prevent it.

Personal protection helps by reducing the amount of dust you inhale. It takes its cheapest form in the dustmask which only works if you do not make much dust, you renew the pads frequently and you are clean-shaven. Respirators are better because they suck air through a series of filters and your face is covered so that you breathe only filtered air. They also protect your face against larger flying objects. I use an Airstream helmet (see Useful Addresses, p. 108) at all times, which incorporates not only dust control and a face shield but also has a hard hat which reduces the impact of flying lumps of wood. As an optional extra it incorporates a pair of ear muffs which rest on the side of the helmet when not in use and can be pulled down when using noisy machinery. Long-term exposure to noise can cause deafness and can be

prevented by this means. Note that these helmets have portable batteries which have to be recharged – but they do run off the mains through a suitably-rated transformer if you do not mind having a lead attached to you.

If you rely solely on personal protection it will be effective against dust only if it is worn at all times in the workshop, because the air will always contain dust. Even if you have not been creating dust on any particular day it will be present on all surfaces, and the small, most dangerous, particles will hang in the air for a long time, supplemented by the slightest movement that causes eddies of air to send more dust into circulation.

There are regulations that are mandatory for dust levels in workshops in many countries and you should make yourself familiar with what is required. In Great Britain, the Health and Safety at Work Act 1974 lays down who is responsible for 'securing the health, safety and welfare of persons at work' and it is clear that this not only includes employers but also the self-employed, and indeed anyone who 'has control of the premises in connection with the carrying on by him of a trade, business or other undertaking (whether for profit or not)'. One of the stated aims is to protect 'persons other than persons at work', which means that if anyone visits your workshop you have a duty to make sure that 'any plant or substance in the premises . . . is safe and without risk to health'.

The Act makes provision for the passing of regulations laying down the substances which must be controlled, and one of these is the Control of Substances Hazardous to Health (COSHH) Regulations 1988 which states 'that after the 1st January 1990, no work which is liable to expose anyone to substances hazardous to health shall be carried on, unless an assessment has been made, by the employer, in relation to evaluating the risk to health arising from the work'. The regulations specify that the amount of hardwood dust shall not exceed five milligrams per cubic metre of air which is a very small amount if you care to work it out, but rather more than the minimum amount that can cause lung damage (two milligrams per cubic metre).

To test this requires specialist equipment but if this is not available the responsibility may be delegated to a reputable firm of dust extraction engineers.

The regulations are monitored by the Health and Safety Executive, but whether their inspectors would have the time or inclination to visit everyone who has a lathe in their shed is open to question. In the United States, the Occupational Safety and Health Administration (OSHA) is responsible for recommending the levels of exposure and the National Institute for Occupational Safety and Health (NIOSH) tests and approves (or otherwise) safety equipment.

What is not in doubt is that the regulations specify a maximum level of dust that the experts think is practicable to maintain, not one that is totally safe. You should therefore aim at keeping well within this limit and most manufacturers of dust extractors will say that their equipment is capable of reducing the levels of dust to one milligram per cubic metre. They will also say, however, that woodturning lathes are the most difficult machines to provide hoods for because the operations carried out on them involve so many different positions and the dust flies out in so many different directions.

There are several manufacturers making many different sizes of extractors rated according to the amount of air they can shift in a given time and the size of particle they filter out. Consult the woodturning press for your nearest suppliers and get a range of quotes in the usual way. It may seem expensive to buy a dust extractor but new lungs are in short supply. Once you have installed one you will never want to be without it because it makes the workshop a much cleaner and therefore more pleasant environment in which to work.

Before you get your extractor you should give some thought as to its eventual position because if you have insufficient height for the standard model, the manufacturers will have to alter it to suit. It should be as close to the source of dust as possible

because the longer the duct the more the air in it is slowed down, rendering it less efficient. The best place is outside the workshop so that any particles that do escape through the filter are carried away in the air. You will need to protect it against the weather and, if you are near neighbours, render it soundproof, for extractors are noisy things. However, while it is most efficient to put the extractor outside it not only removes the dust but also all the warm air. I have resolved this problem by moving the extractor outside in the warm months and inside during the winter.

The duct should be of metal because plastic piping can allow the build-up of static electricity which can create sparks, in turn igniting the dust and possibly causing a nasty explosion. Its diameter should be almost as big as the opening in the extractor. You may think, as I did, that if it is smaller then the air goes faster, but in fact what it does is to reduce the amount of air sucked in and make the motor work harder. What you need is to maximize the throughput and you do this by large, smooth ducting, as short a run as possible and the minimum number of bends.

At the lathe a hood is required to direct the air into the duct. You can buy these ready-made or use a rainwater hopper. I made mine from a 22-litre (5 gallon) drum cut in half. In any case because you will probably find that you make dust at different points along the lathe you should make it easy to adjust.

There will probably be several sources of dust in your workshop, perhaps from a bandsaw as well as from your lathe. By installing storm gates and branch lines in the ducting you can extract the dust from all of these in turn.

Whatever you do about dust extraction you will still get dust on your clothes. It makes no sense to carry this out of the workshop so that you and those nearest to you can continue to breathe it. A boiler suit with velcro fastenings which you keep in the workshop prevents this from happening and it is a good idea to wash exposed skin as soon as you leave the workshop.

GENERAL SAFETY TIPS

● Dangly bits can get caught up in rotating machinery, so avoid wearing anything that might get tangled and drag you towards a horrible fate. Included in this category are loose clothing, jewelry and hair (I always tie mine up before even entering the workshop); and never turn in the buff!

● If anything is going to part company with the lathe, centrifugal force tends to make it fly at right angles to the lathe. Bowls are most prone to do this because of the way they are attached at only one

end, so try to do as much work as possible facing the inside of the bowl. If anything goes wrong and you get sufficient warning to do something about it, retreating from the danger zone is the best policy, so keep an escape route open. When you are safe, you can think what to do to minimize the danger such as switching off the lathe, perhaps by turning off the power supply.

● Before you turn on the lathe, check the speed setting. It is all too easy, particularly with a variable speed model, to turn something small at a fast speed and return to the lathe later to turn something large and not remember the setting. Try to get into the habit of always leaving the lathe set at a slow speed. Always rotate the work by hand before you start the lathe to ensure that it can run freely.

WORKSHOP LAYOUT

Good layout comes with common sense, experience and making the best of what you have. As you can see from **fig. 2** (p. 19), my workshop is not ideal, owing to the small amount of natural light, so the lathe is positioned to take best advantage of what natural light there is. I can easily raise my eyes to look out of the window, which gives my eye muscles an opportunity to relax and my mind an opportunity to

enjoy the garden. There are plenty of work surfaces nearby on which to rest tools and any other equipment. I need to keep tools in their own places so that I can readily lay my hands on them without having to stop and think. I always keep abrasives in piles of the same grade as there is nothing so time-wasting as sorting through a pile of similar-looking sandpaper to find the piece you want.

The nearest piece of machinery to the lathe is the next most frequently used; the bench grinder. It is impossible to over-stress how important it is to keep your tools sharp. I have the bench grinder so close to the lathe that I merely have to turn round to switch it on and sharpen my tool. It is located high on a shelf, at eye-level in fact. This means that I can use it without bending to see if the bevel is rubbing. Everything should be done to save your back from excessive strain.

The bandsaw does not have to be in any particular position in relation to the lathe because the two are not worked in conjunction with one another. It is simply as close to the extractor duct as possible for reasons already discussed and positioned so that I can swing the largest piece of wood possible without re-arranging the furniture.

I have a trestle table in the middle of the room on which to put work in progress. I can easily dismantle it if I need the room. I also have a lot of shelves containing blanks and half-made bowls which I keep in the workshop because it is damp in Devon and I need to keep them as dry as possible – I often have a dehumidifier running in the workshop for this purpose. This has the side effect of raising the background temperature because the drying process releases latent heat.

Most people have to make do with the best they can in terms of their workshop but you must give priority to safety. This really boils down to being careful with the potentially dangerous things such as electricity and dust, providing yourself with enough light to see potential hazards and keeping the place tidy and well organized.

-3-

FURTHER **U**SEFUL **E**QUIPMENT

BENCH GRINDER

The only major piece of equipment you need apart from the lathe, and there is no point in getting a lathe without one, is a bench grinder for sharpening your tools. They are not very expensive, they last for years, and there is no sensible alternative. Do not even consider fitting a stone to your lathe because it will not have guards to reduce the escape of sparks and, if the stone breaks up, to prevent parts of the stone flying out. It is also grossly inefficient to stop turning and remove the work from the lathe to replace it with a stone.

The idea that sharpening your tools means interrupting your turning is to be avoided. Occasional turners should be as conscious of efficiency as full-time turners. If you have a limited time only to spend on an activity, it is very important that you do not waste it; and the most wasteful thing to do is to turn inefficiently because your tool is blunt.

The bevel on a turning tool needs to be concave, so an oilstone will not do. Indeed, I never use one for my turning tools. There are some expensive grindstones on the market that incorporate a whetstone – again these are not so useful to the turner as an ordinary bench grinder because they are too slow.

Most grinders are made to take two wheels. If you use only carbon steel tools one of these can be fine grey and the other coarse grey. High speed steel tools are so good, however, that sooner or later you should get yourself some of these, in which case you will need a soft white aluminium oxide stone 60 to 80 grit size, medium to soft grade K, on the grinder. This will also sharpen carbon steel tools, so the other wheel on the grinder can be a coarse grey stone for removing chips from a carbon steel tool or altering its profile. See Chapter Two (p. 22) for the position of the grinder, and Chapter Four (p. 27–40) on how to use it.

CHAINSAW

When you first start to turn you can get away with not having a power saw if you purchase your wood already cut. If you are not committed to the craft this is probably better than investing in a power saw, but wood cut into bowl blanks is costly because the supplier has to bear the cost of cutting it plus the waste that is inherent in cutting out blanks. However, if you bought a whole plank, you could use the offcuts.

Of all my power saws, the one I should least like to lose is the chainsaw. It is so versatile that I can cut down trees, cut logs into rough planks and cut planks into roughly circular blanks. Because the shaping is done on the lathe, precisely cut blanks are not normally necessary. The main exception to this is some spindle turning, such as balusters, where the design may incorporate some square-sectioned parts which must be planed before the piece is turned, to ensure that the turned parts are on the same axis as the square parts. I must stress, however, that **chainsaws are incredibly dangerous** and must not be used without training and the correct safety gear.

If you hire a chainsaw you should already have taken a course on how to use it and you should have your own safety equipment as advised on that course. Hire firms have a responsibility to satisfy these requirements but they often do not. It's your body – so look after it.

Just in case you need reminding, I will give a brief resumé of some safety tips. Always wear a helmet with face protector and ear muffs in place, along with steel tipped boots, gloves and special trousers. Make sure that the wood is secured firmly before you start, never work with the saw above shoulder height and make sure that no one is standing anywhere near you when you are sawing.

Wedges are vital tools to use with your chainsaw because they keep the cut open, allowing the saw to cut cleanly without the wood binding it. Plastic is the best material, or you can make your own out of wood, but iron wedges are not kind to the saw and can be dangerous. You will sometimes find that you can split the wood more easily than cut it

– a great fuel- and time-saver if the wood is suitable.

If you decide to buy a chainsaw, do make sure that it has all the safety features possible, especially a chain brake that stops the saw instantly in case of kick back.

There are two types of chainsaw, petrol or electric. A petrol saw can be used away from a power source and is thus better suited to cutting down trees. It will also tend to be proportionately more powerful than an electric model. On the debit side it is more noisy, more smelly, and requires more maintenance, and you cannot use a petrol model in a confined space as the fumes are deadly. Therefore I have one of each: a large petrol model for cutting down trees and for cutting large bits of tree into manageable lumps, and a smaller electric one for use near to and within the workshop.

BANDSAW

If you do a lot of faceplate work a bandsaw is essential for cutting the blanks. I suggest that you go for a model with the greatest depth of cut that you can afford. The other relevant specification is width of cut, which is determined by the distance between the blade and the body of the saw. You might at first think that you need a saw with the same width of cut as the maximum size you can turn, but in fact it can be less

than that since the whole of your blank does not need to be between the blade and the body. Saws with only two band wheels are superior to those with three because the blade does not have to travel through such acute angles, which causes them to break relatively quickly.

The type of blade most suitable for cutting blanks upwards of 100cm (4in) in diameter is 12cm ($\frac{1}{2}$in) wide. The tooth format I recommend is 3 skip which does not bind in deep cuts, especially in wet wood, as much as blades with a higher tooth pitch.

This is another tool that can easily injure, so keep your fingers away from the blade while it is going round. When cutting small items, push them towards the blade with a stick cut from waste wood so that your fingers do not go near the blade. Never cut anything that overhangs as the blade will snatch it – and whether you end up with a buckled blade or a piece of wood hurtling through the air is a matter of luck! When pushing your wood towards the blade avoid doing so with your hand or fingers on the line you hope to be cutting, because the wood can suddenly either cut faster than you expect, or split, and your forward momentum may carry your hand on to the blade.

SMALL TOOLS

You will probably find that most of the small tools you need are already in your tool kit: e.g. screwdrivers, a hammer, rulers, bradawl, electric drill and so on. There are some more specialized tools that you will find useful such as callipers, both internal and external, which I will introduce at the appropriate place in the book.

READING MATTER AND COURSES

Magazines are a useful source of information on techniques, product reviews, inspirational articles by luminaries of the trade and advertisements, both by the trade and private individuals, for second-hand tools. I include a list of magazines in the back along with a list of recommended books.

You can learn a lot by spending time with an expert who also knows how to teach, but it is difficult to choose your course because there are no nationally-agreed standards of teaching, despite the best efforts of the National Associations to instigate them. All I can suggest is that you read magazines and books to see whose ideas appeal to you, and see if they will teach you. Your friends in the local woodturning club will be able to advise. However, be warned that you must be prepared to pay for your lessons, at least as much as you have to pay the plumber or music teacher, for we all have to live.

The pieces of equipment described in this section can be accumulated gradually as you need them, so you do not need to buy them all as soon as you start except for the grindstone which is absolutely vital.

—4——

TOOLS AND SHARPENING

CHOICE OF TOOLS

Buy tools only as you need them and avoid sets as they always contain tools you never use. There are two basic types of tool: gouges and chisels. Gouges have a semi-circular cross-section and a channel running down part of their length; chisels have a rectangular cross-section. Turning tools differ from other woodworking tools in so far as they are generally made of thicker material and have longer tangs (the bit that goes in the handle) and longer handles. The thickness is mainly so that the tools can stand up to the stresses imparted by the downward thrust of the wood against the static rest, but it also absorbs the heat generated by the friction of the wood.

The long tangs make the junction between metal and wood more secure and the long handles give greater leverage. Do not be carried away by the fashion for extremely long handles as they are not really necessary for 'normal' turning and serve only to make you think that great

force is necessary. I hope to show that it is not.

Some of the tools I use are carving tools. Where great leverage is not required there is no necessity for the long handles and thick steel of purpose-made turning tools. Indeed, the short handles and finer shapes of carving tools are a positive advantage in some cases. I am strongly of the opinion that it does not really matter what tool you use to get the effect you want as long as it is safe. Certain tools are less effective than others and those who choose to use them may be wasting their time, but that is their concern.

Making your own tools from some old bit of metal can be quite rewarding, I am told, but I am much more interested in wood-turning. If you do take up this branch of metalworking do ensure that you know what exactly makes a good wood-turning tool in terms of general construction and more particularly the correct type of steel. I am not qualified to advise on this but I would suggest that you avoid the sort of steel that files are made of,

since their specifications require hardness whereas turning tools require a degree of elasticity. You do not want a tool that may snap under pressure.

I have already mentioned carbon and high speed steel. They require different sharpening stones because the latter is much harder than the former. They cost about a third as much again, but they are definitely worth it for the serious turner because they hold their edge twice as long and therefore last twice as long.

Most turners make their own handles partly because they are mean and have the wood anyway but also because they can make each handle different so they are readily identifiable when poking out of a pile of shavings (**fig. 3**).

Overleaf is a set of tools that you will need to get started: I describe how to use them in Part Two.

SHARPENING – INTRODUCTION

All these tools need a concave bevel, which is created by the

Fig. 3
Tools in pile of shavings

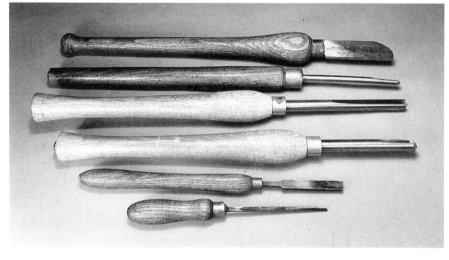

Set of bowl turning tools, from the top:

37.5mm ($1\frac{1}{2}$in) wide, 9.37mm ($\frac{3}{8}$in) section, half round scraper

6.25mm ($\frac{1}{4}$in) deep fluted bowl gouge

12.5mm ($\frac{1}{2}$in) deep fluted bowl gouge, straight across

12.5mm ($\frac{1}{2}$in) deep fluted bowl gouge, ground back

12.5mm ($\frac{1}{2}$in) wide, 6.25mm ($\frac{1}{4}$in) section, scraper

6.25mm ($\frac{1}{4}$in) shallow carving gouge

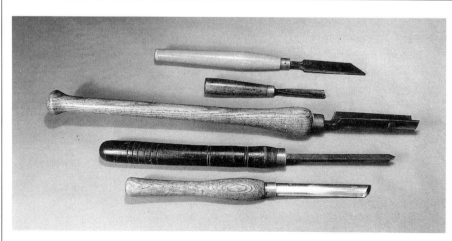

Set of spindle tools, from the top:

fluted parting tool

12.5mm ($\frac{1}{2}$in) spindle (carving) gouge

31.25mm ($1\frac{1}{4}$in) roughing gouge

9.37mm ($\frac{3}{8}$in) beading and parting tool

18.75mm ($\frac{3}{4}$in) oval skew chisel

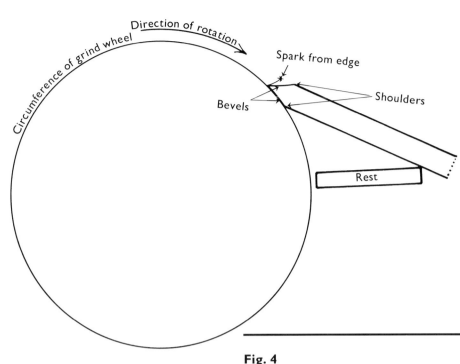

Fig. 4
Concave bevel, sharpening parting tool

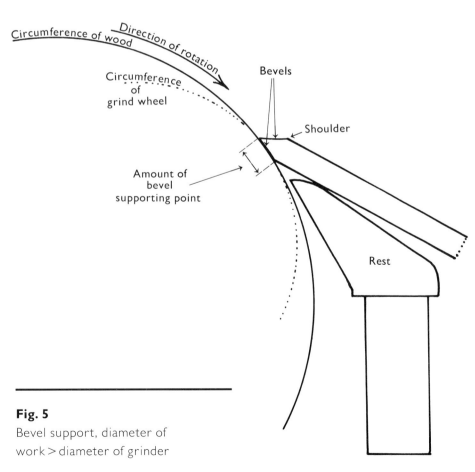

Fig. 5
Bevel support, diameter of
work > diameter of grinder

grinder **(fig. 4)**. The main reason why turning tools do not dig in is because the edge is supported by some part of the bevel. If the bevel is convex and you are turning a convex curve (the outside of a bowl or a cylinder) the only part of the bevel that can rub is just behind the edge and there is not enough distance between these points to give much stability.

This concave bevel is created by the rim of the grinding wheel. Only when the diameter of the wheel is the same as or smaller than the circumference of the work, will it produce a bevel such that a cut with the tool edge at right angles to the circumference of the work will produce the maximum support (ie. at the ridge where bevel and tool surface meet) **(fig. 5)**. If the diameter of the wheel is larger than the work and the tool is presented at right angles, the edge will be supported by a point on the bevel nearer to the edge and so the support is less stable **(fig. 6, overleaf)**.

If, however, you rotate the tool so that it is presented at an angle smaller than 90°, you will see that the ridge and the edge can be made to rub at the same time (you can check this out by holding the tool against a cylinder with a light source behind). In Chapter Six you will find that this position means that the edge and bevel are not on the same circumference of the work. However, if you maintain the angle, the tool is pulled by the rotation of the wood in the same direction that the edge overhangs the bevel **(fig. 7)**.

Most professionals use the tool straight from the grinder, with no other sharpening or honing necessary. If you hone the edge on a whetstone you get a very sharp edge, but this does not last long because of the friction of the wood, and is usually a waste of time. Indeed, honing the edge does tend to flatten the bevel.

There are no hard and fast rules about the angles of bevels, as it depends on your height and personal preference. However with a very long bevel, while you can achieve a very fine edge, it will rapidly heat up and become blunt, and it is also more difficult to get the bevel to support the edge. At the other extreme a very short bevel will produce an edge that lasts a long time but does not cut so cleanly. You need small tools for small diameter work as the thinness of the metal gives a sharp edge but a short bevel which conforms more nearly to the diameter of the work.

Sharp tools are essential to get a clean cut and if you do not cut cleanly then you need to spend more time finishing. If you allow the edge to become blunt you have to change the angle of the tool to get it to cut at all, and this means you move further away from the safe angle. You also start to use more force than you ought to to get the tool to cut. Both these actions can lead to accidents, so, when you feel that this might be happening, stop and look at the tool edge. If light reflects from the edge, then it is

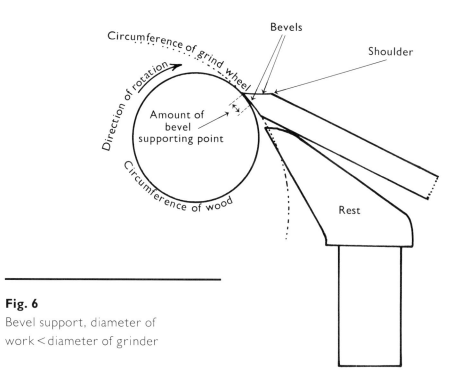

Fig. 6
Bevel support, diameter of
work < diameter of grinder

blunt. Another visual clue is the presence of gunge sticking to the steel. This effect varies from wood to wood and also becomes more pronounced with wet woods. A sharp edge leaves no residue because the fibres are cut so cleanly that they speed away from the tool without leaving a trace.

The problem when you start turning is that you simply do not know what a sharp tool is like to work with. When you take the brand new tools out of their bag, they are not sharp, and they might be the first turning tools you have ever owned. Not only do you not know how to sharpen tools but you may never have seen a sharp tool. I can tell you how to sharpen tools as clearly as I can but it needs practice, and by the time you have practised on your new tool you have lost

the original shape and there may not be much steel left at all.

I know when you get a new tool you are desperate to use it, but if you can restrain yourself, I suggest you practise sharpening on an old chisel. Why not sharpen that old one you used for some totally inappropriate function until its edge resembled a mountain range? Try to give it one bevel like a scraper and you will probably find a use for it eventually, if there is any steel left.

First, check the trueness of the stone. If it has any ridges or hollows, or has a discoloured surface due to the presence of ingrained dirt or tool steel, it needs dressing with a dressing tool. **Fig. 8** shows how to do this if the stone is not dramatically distorted. If it causes the dressing tool to bounce around then you

Fig. 7
Effect of edge overhanging bevel

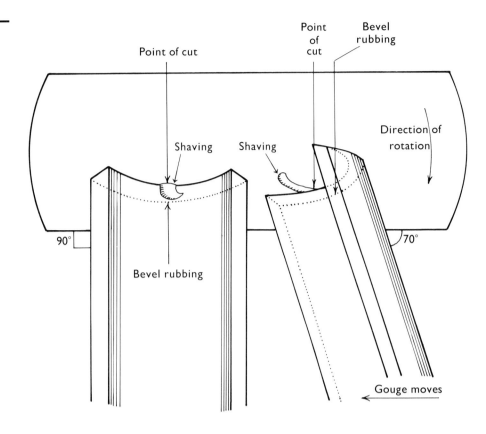

Fig. 8
Starwheel stone dresser

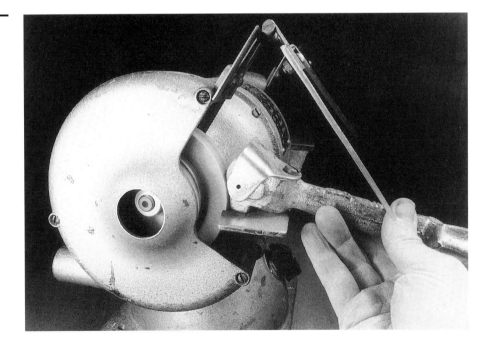

will have to move the rest away from the stone so that you can hang the lugs on the bottom of the tool over the rest, to enable the tool to be held against the stone with more pressure. Dressing tools are not expensive and if your stone is not regular you cannot expect your edge to be.

Sharpening the scraper is the first technique to be described in this book, and I shall preface it with a homily about the mental attitude to adopt before starting something, in the hope that it will become a habit with you: **before you do anything, think safety**.

Is the grindstone properly guarded and are you wearing your eye protection? Is there anything on the floor that you might trip on? Think through what you are going to do like a high jumper at the Olympic games, and physically go through the motions without the grindstone turning so that you know what you are going to do, where you will start and where you will end up. An experienced operator knows how he will be standing at the end of an operation without thinking about it and assumes a stance at the beginning which enables him to complete the action without losing balance. That is why they look so smooth and why they do not fall over.

SCRAPERS

Sharpening an old chisel to convert it to a scraper is not so complicated that you are likely to fall over but the principle is worth remembering. All you will need to do in this instance is ensure that the whole of the rim of the stone contacts the edge of the chisel evenly. Most tools are wider than the stone, so this necessitates passing the tool from side to side along the tool rest so that the stone grinds an equal amount off every part of the chisel.

You are going to have to remove the chips in the edge of the scraper before you can establish the required bevel, so it does not matter what angle you work at until this is achieved. Since you are going to be removing a lot of metal you will probably heat up the tool even though you are using the coarse stone and not pressing hard. So get yourself a pot of water to cool the tool down frequently before it turns blue, which shows that it is losing its temper.

Now you know what you are going to do you can start the grinder. First of all remove the old chipped edge by pushing the tool against the grinder with the tool flat on the rest (**fig. 9**). When you have removed the old edge you will have two bevels or perhaps one at a right angle. You are aiming to make an edge on the tool so that the angle between the top surface and the bevel is about 60°. This is steeper even than abused carpentry chisels but is probably less steep than your old chisel when you have removed the old edge. You must therefore lower the handle of the tool so that the edge goes higher on the stone and the bevel can be ground back (**fig. 10**).

Start with the edge pointing upwards and with the shoulder (the junction between bevel and tool surface, see **figs. 4–6**, p. 29–30), not the edge, in contact with the stone. Grind up towards the edge checking that you are making the required bevel angle. At first you will have two bevels (**fig. 11, overleaf**), but as you continue, the bottom bevel will overtake the top one and eventually reach the edge (**fig. 12, overleaf**), at which point sparks will appear over the edge as in **fig. 4**, p. 29. You should aim to have a smooth bevel, not a many facetted affair. Because the stone should be running at right angles to the edge of the tool, the lines left by the stone should also be aligned this way.

You can now scrutinize the quality of the edge, which is ideally as thin as possible. The test is to look for bright lights; in other words, hold the edge so that the light shines on it and if there are any reflections it is clearly thicker than it should be. If you have had to do a lot of grinding you will have caused a burr to form on the edge which may confuse the way the light reflects. This can be removed by rubbing the top of the tool surface with a whetstone or pulling the edge through a piece of soft wood. You will then be able to see the edge more clearly. Some people believe that this burr does the cutting when you use a scraper. In my experience

Fig. 9
Old chisel, flat on rest

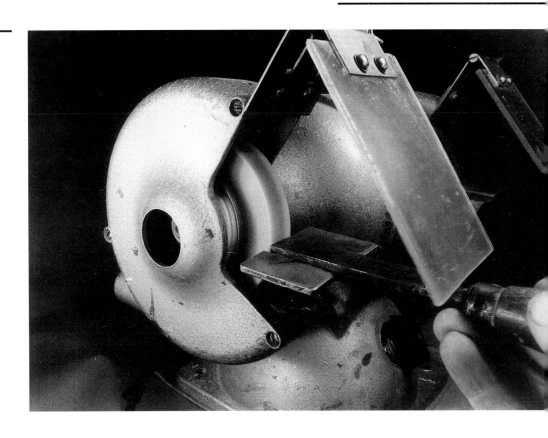

Fig. 10
Old chisel, grinding bevel back

the burr lasts no time at all when pushed against a piece of rotating wood so I grind my scrapers at a less steep angle and rely on the cutting edge so produced.

BEADING AND PARTING CHISELS

The next easiest tool to sharpen is the beading and parting tool (see figs. 4–6, p. 29–30). The difference between this and the scraper is the presence of two bevels. Because the tool is narrower than the stone you do not have to move it from side to side. Sharpen one bevel until you reach the edge and then turn the tool over and do the other side. The main problem is to maintain the edge at right angles to the tool, which you should find easy to do if the stone is true and you align the tool so that its length is in a straight line with the sides of the stone.

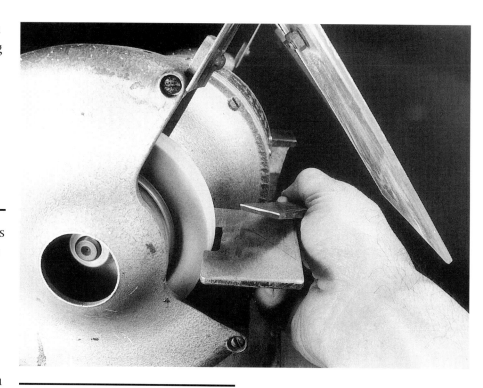

Fig. 11
Old chisel, two bevels

Fig. 12
Old chisel, one bevel

SKEW CHISELS (fig. 13)

The skew chisel is almost as easy
to sharpen as the beading and
parting tool except that to
maintain the angle of the skew
you have to hold the tool at an
angle to the stone, so that the
edge is more or less parallel to the
rim of the stone **(fig. 14)**. Once
you have established this angle
you must keep the same angle as
you pass the tool along the rest.
This requires that you move the
end of the handle at the same rate
as the edge.

As you will see in Chapter Six,
I use a curved skew chisel. This
is not very different to sharpen
than a straight skew **(fig. 15,
overleaf)**. You achieve this shape
in the first place by grinding the
bevel on both sides at the heel of
the tool, so that you end up with
a edge that comes to a point half
way along **(fig. 16, overleaf)**.
When all four bevels are the same
width you can then grind the
point in the middle **(fig. 17,
overleaf)** to get a curve **(fig. 19,
overleaf)**. Grind this smooth
curve by moving the tool in a
smooth arc maintaining the same
angle all the time.

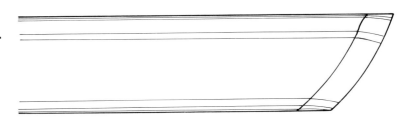

Fig. 13
Oval skew chisel 18.75mm (¾in)

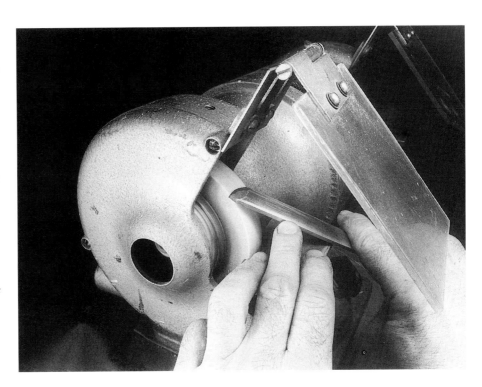

Fig. 14
Skew, angle of edge at stone

Fig. 15
Skew, straight edged

Fig. 16
Skew, grinding away straight edge

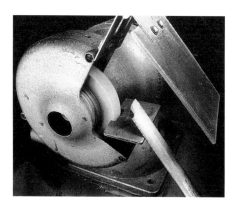

Fig. 17
Skew, grinding away point

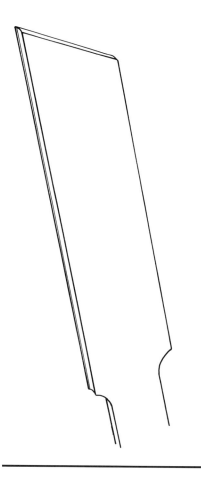

Fig. 18
Fluted parting tool

Fig. 19
Skew, curved edge attained

ROUGHING GOUGES (fig. 20)

The easiest gouge to sharpen is the roughing gouge. Instead of moving the tool along the rest, as in the case of the scraper, the tool remains in the same place and you roll the tool over so that the whole bevel rubs against the stone in a single smooth movement. This movement can only be achieved if you hold the tool handle at the start of the roll with your wrist twisted to one extreme, so that when you have finished the roll your wrist has turned to the other extreme. If you practise this movement before you start the grinder you will be able to master it before you endanger the tool. During this roll the axis of the tool should be parallel to the side of the stone at all times.

BOWL GOUGES (figs. 24–25)

Bowl gouges are sometimes supplied with an edge which is ground straight across (**fig. 24**). I use both this pattern and one with the bevel running down the sides (**fig. 25**). The first is similar to the roughing gouge to sharpen; you keep the tool in the same alignment during the process and just roll it from side to side (**figs. 26–29**).

The gouge shown in fig. 25 is the most difficult tool to sharpen. Starting with the tool as supplied, you need to grind back the

Fig. 20
Roughing gouge 31.25mm (1¼in)

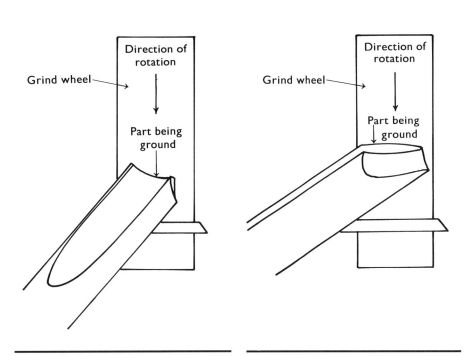

Fig. 21
Grinding ground-back-gouge, left of bevel

Fig. 22
Grinding ground-back-gouge, halfway along left bevel

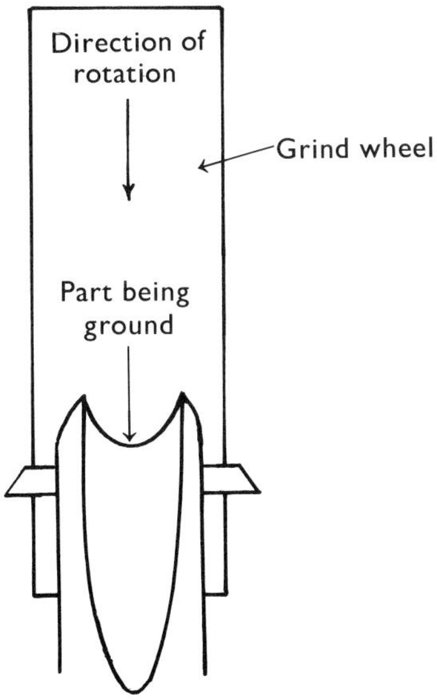

Fig. 24
Deep fluted bowl gouge, straight-across 12.5mm (½in)

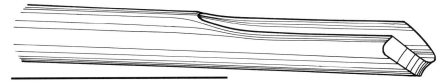

Fig. 23
Grinding ground-back-gouge, point of bevel

Fig. 25
Deep fluted bowl gouge, ground-back 12.5mm (½in)

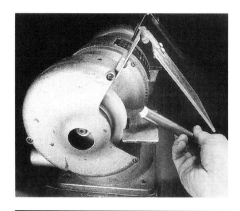

Fig. 26
Deep-fluted bowl gouge as supplied

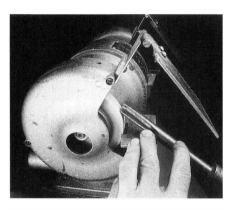

Fig. 27
Deep-fluted bowl gouge, sharpening
straight across

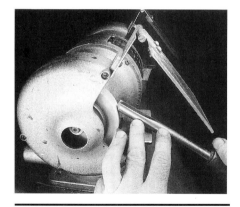

Fig. 28
Deep-fluted bowl gouge, sharpening
straight across

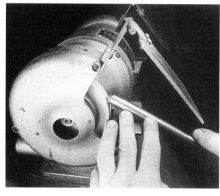

Fig. 29
Deep-fluted bowl gouge, sharpening
straight across

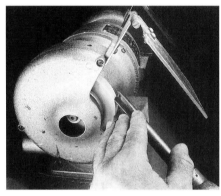

Fig. 30
Deep-fluted bowl gouge, grinding
back bevel

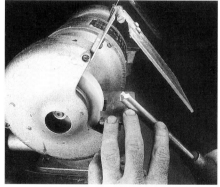

Fig. 31
Deep-fluted bowl gouge, bevel with
point

wings. Do both sides with the edge parallel to the rim of the stone and 45° to the vertical (**fig. 30**). When you have ground back both sides, with the edge of the tool parallel to the rest, and so that the bevel on the sides is the same angle as the original bevel, you will have two points on each side which need to be ground away (**fig. 31**).

You are merging the side bevels into the old bevel near the centre, so this requires some delicacy and frequent stops to inspect what you have achieved. Start by grinding at the point and then swinging the tool in an ever greater arc either side of this point. **Fig. 32** shows the bevels partly merged and **fig. 33** shows the bevels on one side completely merged with the centre bevel. Now the other side needs to be done.

When you come to sharpen the tool subsequently you will have to swing it right from one side of the grinder to the other because you have to sharpen the entire edge even though it may be only blunt at one point, otherwise you will lose the profile of the tool. Try a dry run of this action before you turn on the grinder and you will see that you can only achieve it in one motion by standing back so that the tool passes between your body and the grinder. Some of us need to stand farther from the grinder than others to make this space!

You will also have to grip the tool in such a way that you can smoothly alter your grip throughout the movement. For

Fig. 32
Deep-fluted bowl gouge, bevel point
partly ground away

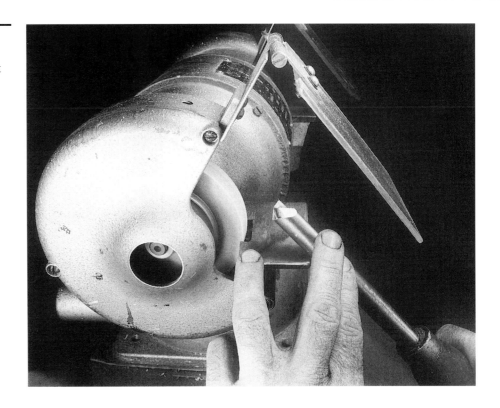

Fig. 33
Deep-fluted bowl gouge, bevel point
gone

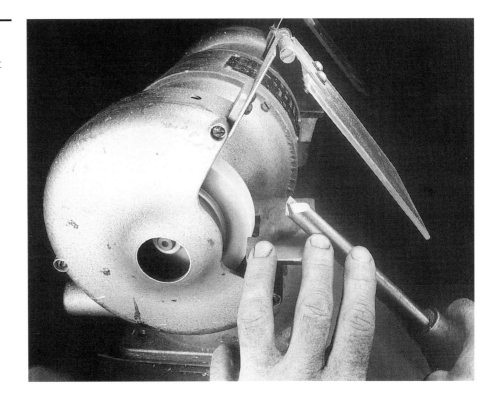

someone using their right hand on the end of the handle, this means starting off with the right hand gripping over the handle at the right hand extreme of the arc, and finishing on the left hand extreme with an underhand grip. All the time the other hand is gripping the tool at the rest and you are also trying to keep the bevel at the same angle to the stone. Because of the complexity of the shape the smooth arc from one side to the other does not stay in one plane. You have to raise the handle gradually as you approach the point where you are sharpening the end of the tool, and as you pass this point, gradually lower it again **(see figs. 21–23, p. 37)**.

Sharpening tools correctly is certainly a difficult art to learn but it is absolutely essential. You can have the best lathe in the world in the ideal workshop, a beautiful piece of timber and an exquisite design in your head, but if your tools are not sharp you will not be able to produce a good piece of work. If you think your tool is blunt, it will be, so sharpen it.

—5

WOOD

HARDWOODS AND SOFTWOODS

The first thing you should know about wood is that it comes from a tree, and that tree produced it to support its branches and carry nutrients to its leaves. The tree may well have lived for upwards of 50 years, providing a home for countless millions of other organisms and contributing to the environment by consolidating carbon dioxide and producing oxygen and water to add to the atmosphere.

You owe it to the tree to do something equally as beautiful and useful with its body.

Trees are divided botanically into hardwoods and softwoods, a distinction which is made on the basis of the structure of their seeds, though in practice they divide neatly into deciduous and coniferous (evergreen) types respectively. While this distinction often coincides with their relative hardness, it does not necessarily follow: for example, the softest wood, balsa, is actually a hardwood and one of the harder woods, yew, is a softwood.

STRUCTURE

The key to understanding the structure of wood lies in remembering its original purpose, which is to carry liquids up and down the trunk. It can do this because it consists of hollow vessels that run the length of the tree and, for the purposes of demonstrating its cutting characteristics, can be usefully likened to a bundle of straws. If you tape about twenty-four drinking straws together (fig. 34) and try the two diametrically opposite ways of cutting it, you will see that the downward thrust is cutting with the grain and the upwards thrust is cutting against the grain. As you can see in fig. 35, the straws compress when the edge is pressed against them because the straws underneath support the straws being cut. This means that the straws that are cut are cut cleanly and the underlying ones are not torn. If you attempt to cut wood as in fig. 36, however, the straws that are going to be cut are not supported by anything and are torn away from their neighbours before they are cut. No one

would think of sharpening a pencil as in fig. 36 for that very reason and it is equally bad practice to turn in this direction.

The secret of cutting wood cleanly is to do it in such a way that the fibres you are cutting are always supported. This is what is meant by cutting with the grain, cutting downhill, or, as Frank Pain said in his classic book *The Practical Woodturner*: 'cutting the wood as it would like to be cut'. I always have a problem with this quote because, given a choice, I daresay that the wood would prefer not to be cut, but that is by the by.

During the course of a growing season a tree increases its size by making more layers of 'straws' just under the bark (the cambium layer). It therefore builds up its bulk around a central core and its season's growth can be seen in the form of rings. The rings near the outside of the tree carry the water and nutrients from the roots to the leaves and are called sapwood. The sapwood is sometimes a different colour to the heartwood (which is essentially dead), as in yew where the heartwood is orange-brown and the sapwood white. During the growing season the sapwood is full of water and trees should not be felled at this time because, being at its wettest, the wood takes longer to dry. It also contains a large amount of nutritious sap which fungi find immensely to their taste and wherein they develop at an alarming rate. In other words, rot sets in. Some woods suffer more than others if they have been summer-felled: sycamore is one of the worst and as a result it soon loses its whiteness and softens apace.

Heartwood is no longer concerned with the upward transport of water to the leaves and so normally has a lower water content than the sapwood; though in some species such as the hickories it may have a higher water content. It is subject to compression from the sapwood and may contain anti-fungal agents, although these can be leached out in some conditions. When these agents are not present the heartwood of an old tree is subject to rot and that is why the inside of an old tree may be discoloured, as in ash, and eventually disappear.

There are other differences of texture within the wood that are not so obvious, but they do have to be borne in mind when processing the tree. When a tree grows on a slope, or when a branch is subject to gravitational forces that tend to make it bend more than is usual, it will produce different types of cells which work to correct these

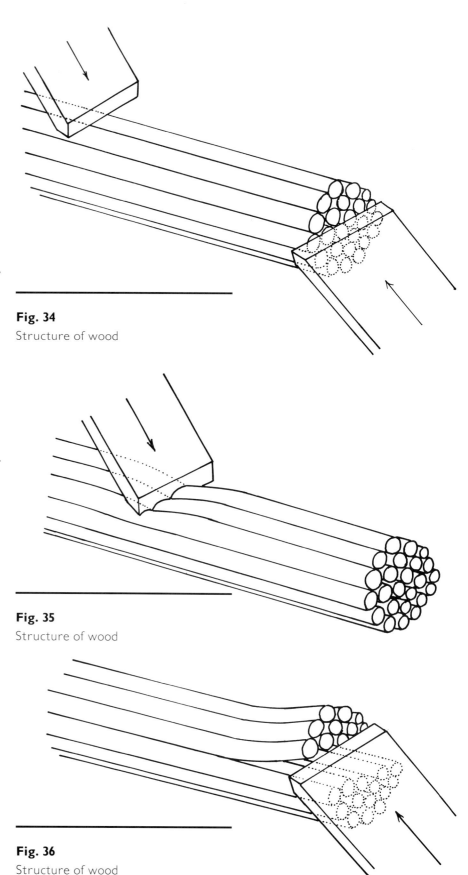

Fig. 34
Structure of wood

Fig. 35
Structure of wood

Fig. 36
Structure of wood

forces. This 'reaction' wood tends to shrink more longitudinally and less transversely than 'normal' wood and so if it is present within a plank will make that plank warp and crack more than usual. This is why the commercial sawyer will cut the crutches off trees and why you should expect a tree with a markedly off-centre heart to distort a lot while drying.

The purpose of bark is to protect the wood against the ravages of insect and beast who would eat it, and the desiccating effect of wind and sun.

EFFECTS OF CHANGES IN MOISTURE CONTENT

When a tree is cut down the ends of the straws are exposed and start to dry out. As they dry they shrink and, because the wood away from the cut edge does not dry as quickly, it remains the same size, resulting in cracks appearing in the end of the tree. This differential shrinkage rate determined by the conditions of exposure is the key to drying cracks or 'shakes'. If you can equalize the exposure you can eliminate the cracks. This is why thin-turned bowls do not crack as they dry. As you may have noticed, however, they do warp.

If you cut the tree into slices, leaving the bark on, water races out of the ends because the tubes are exposed, but not out of the sides because the bark is performing its protective

function. So the ends crack and the cracks tend to travel inwards (longitudinally) along the grain as it dries. The cracks will be wider on the outer rings because the outer rings are longer than the inner ones and so the same percentage loss of volume in their case results in a larger actual loss. The cracks tend to join together along lines of weakness between the tubes and so you get radial shakes. If you cut a newly felled tree into short slices and leave it in the sun it will very soon crack into small pieces. This is why a tree feller cuts trees in the autumn and leaves them in pieces that are as long as possible.

The extent to which wood shrinks when it dries depends on the position occupied by the piece of wood within the tree. Shrinkage around the more or less concentric annular rings is greater than across them radially from the heart to the outside of the log. This means that boards cut tangentially shrink more in width than those cut radially. A tree can be planked either 'through and through' (see diagram) in which case all the boards apart from the centre board are tangential, or it can be 'quarter sawn' (see diagram) in which case all the boards are radial. The former is much more common because it is easier for the mill and there is less initial timber wastage. The latter is harder to do, produces less cubic capacity of wood and narrower planks but the planks display more figure and are more stable as they dry.

All boards shrink more across the grain than along the length and this directly affects the turner because if you cut a circle out of an unseasoned board it will go oval as it dries.

Wood must, however, be dried before it is used because it needs to be stable after it has been turned and because when it has less than a 20 per cent moisture content fungus cannot attack it.

All bodies of air that are comfortable to live in contain some water in the form of water vapour. This is expressed as a percentage and is called the relative humidity. If a piece of wood is left in a room that has a lower relative humidity than the wood does, it will lose moisture and will therefore change in volume. In a room where the relative humidity is higher than the wood it will absorb water, but this happens relatively slowly and is not a common problem.

Both these scenarios lead to a change in shape which is probably not desirable if the wood happens to be a piece you have just turned. That is why you should try to ensure that the wood you turn has a similar moisture content to the air of the room it is going to live in. This requires instrumentation that is not available to everyone so, as a general guide, you can assume that a centrally heated room will have a relative humidity of approximately 50 per cent and that the wood needs to contain 8–10 per cent moisture to be stable in that environment (**fig. 37**).

Traditionally dried timber will

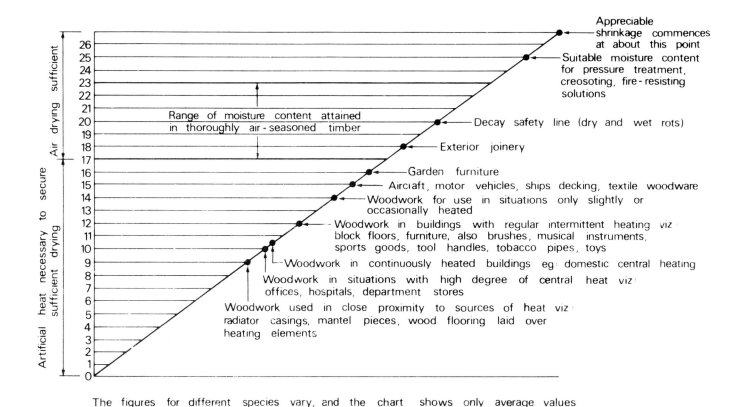

Moisture contents of timber in various environments

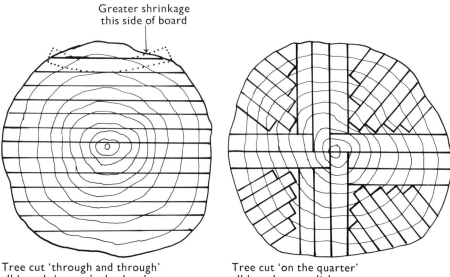

Tree cut 'through and through' all boards 'waney' edged and all boards tangential except centre board.

Tree cut 'on the quarter' all boards are radial

Fig. 37

Tables of moisture content and shrinkage, reproduced from Building Research Establishment Technical Note no. 46 by permission of the controller of HMSO: Crown Copyright 1992

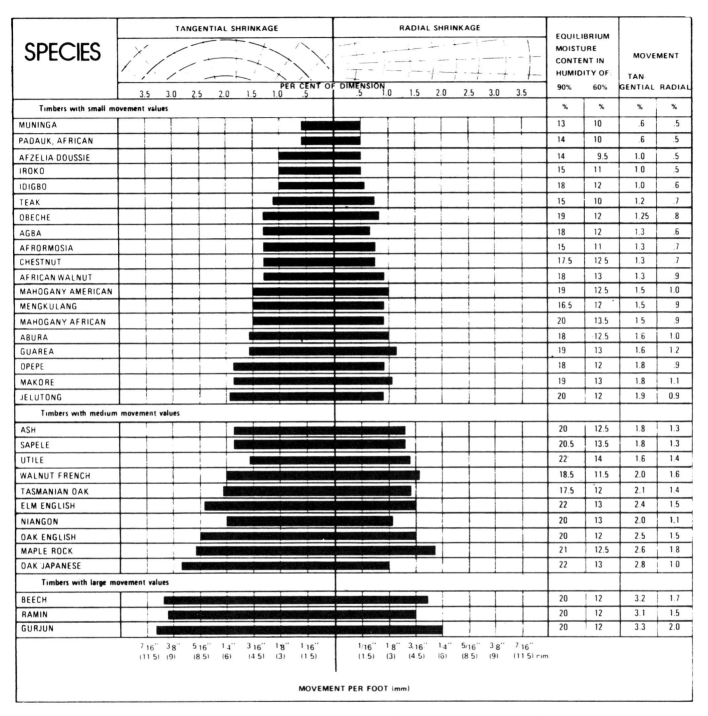

SPECIES	TANGENTIAL SHRINKAGE	RADIAL SHRINKAGE	EQUILIBRIUM MOISTURE CONTENT IN HUMIDITY OF: 90%	60%	MOVEMENT TANGENTIAL	RADIAL
			%	%	%	%
Timbers with small movement values						
MUNINGA			13	10	.6	.5
PADAUK, AFRICAN			14	10	.6	.5
AFZELIA-DOUSSIE			14	9.5	1.0	.5
IROKO			15	11	1.0	.5
IDIGBO			18	12	1.0	.6
TEAK			15	10	1.2	.7
OBECHE			19	12	1.25	.8
AGBA			18	12	1.3	.6
AFRORMOSIA			15	11	1.3	.7
CHESTNUT			17.5	12.5	1.3	.7
AFRICAN WALNUT			18	13	1.3	.9
MAHOGANY AMERICAN			19	12.5	1.5	1.0
MENGKULANG			16.5	12	1.5	.9
MAHOGANY AFRICAN			20	13.5	1.5	.9
ABURA			18	12.5	1.6	1.0
GUAREA			19	13	1.6	1.2
OPEPE			18	12	1.8	.9
MAKORE			19	13	1.8	1.1
JELUTONG			20	12	1.9	0.9
Timbers with medium movement values						
ASH			20	12.5	1.8	1.3
SAPELE			20.5	13.5	1.8	1.3
UTILE			22	14	1.6	1.4
WALNUT FRENCH			18.5	11.5	2.0	1.6
TASMANIAN OAK			17.5	12	2.1	1.4
ELM ENGLISH			22	13	2.4	1.5
NIANGON			20	13	2.0	1.1
OAK ENGLISH			20	12	2.5	1.5
MAPLE ROCK			21	12.5	2.6	1.8
OAK JAPANESE			22	13	2.8	1.0
Timbers with large movement values						
BEECH			20	12	3.2	1.7
RAMIN			20	12	3.1	1.5
GURJUN			20	12	3.3	2.0

PER CENT OF DIMENSION

3.5 3.0 2.5 2.0 1.5 1.0 .5 .5 1.0 1.5 2.0 2.5 3.0 3.5

7/16" (11.5) 3/8" (9) 5/16" (8.5) 1/4" (6) 3/16" (4.5) 1/8" (3) 1/16" (1.5) 1/16" (1.5) 1/8" (3) 3/16" (4.5) 1/4" (6) 5/16" (8.5) 3/8" (9) 7/16" (11.5) rim

MOVEMENT PER FOOT (mm)

Movement of timbers in seasoned condition due to reduced humidity

only be as dry as the air in which it dried, which in temperate climes may mean that the minimum relative humidity is no lower than 17 per cent and is more likely to be higher. The chart on p. 45 shows the amount of movement you can expect in a variety of timbers when the moisture content is reduced from 19 to 12 per cent. As you will see, even in the most stable of timbers there is still a considerable amount of movement at these levels.

SEASONING

The easiest way of measuring the moisture content of the wood is to use a moisture metre. These are quite expensive so an alternative way which takes longer but is more accurate is to carefully weigh a small sample of the wood taken at least 22.5cm (9in) from the end of a plank. Make a note of this weight (it is a good idea to write the weight on the wood itself) and then dry it. The best way to dry it is to put it in the oven or the airing cupboard. Do this until its weight is stable. If you weigh the wood again and express the difference in percentage terms you will have the moisture content. If the sample weighs 8 units and the dry weight is 7 units then the moisture content is one-seventh of the dry weight, that is approximately 14 per cent.

The traditional way of avoiding degradation while

drying is to cut the tree into longitudinal slices (planks) at the beginning of the winter when it will be exposed to fewest extremes of temperature and humidity. It is then protected from the sun and rain but exposed to all available draughts for as long as possible. This is achieved by stacking the planks in a suitable shed, in the same order that they were removed from the tree but on bearers of say 10cm (4in) square-section, with laths of wood approximately 18.75mm ($\frac{3}{4}$in) square-section between each plank and spaced at intervals of 90cm (3ft).

Thin planks obviously dry quicker than thick ones and because they dry more evenly should crack less. The rate of drying is generally estimated at 12 months per 25mm (1in) of board thickness, though in practice this varies with the original wetness of the wood, the atmospheric conditions it is stored under and the species.

Planks over 50mm (2in) thick take proportionately longer to dry and over 10cm (4in) may not dry all the way through at all. This is because the outer layer may dry but the water contained in the centre may be unable to migrate to the outside. This happens particularly when the drying process is speeded up too quickly.

I am particularly fortunate in my wood storing facilities, having an enclosed area where it is always cool and shady and not exposed to drying winds, where I can store wood that is already

dry, or wood that is wet and required to dry very slowly. I also have a drying shed which has a closed wall facing south to keep off the sun, side walls of restricted access so that the wind does not howl through but there is some movement of air, and an open front facing north that allows good air circulation but no sun (**fig. 38**). Naturally, it also has a roof to keep off the rain.

BUYING TIMBER

I acquired the facilities detailed above only after turning for many years, so when I started turning I had to buy wood that had been dried by someone else. I soon learned that my definition of dry wood differed from that of the people I was buying from. Unless you buy wood from an exceptionally responsible source, which means that it will be expensive, you must find out the moisture content of the wood for yourself and be prepared to dry it before you use it.

The great advantage that turners have over most timber users is that you can use short pieces, provided you know how to deal with them and look after them. This means that you can take advantage of fallen or felled trees that are too small or unfavourably placed for commercial timber dealers to be interested in them. Quite small exotic trees that are grown in the garden, such as laburnum, robinia, and any of the fruit

Fig. 38
Drying shed

woods, can yield interesting timber for just the cost of fetching them. I do strongly recommend that you give the owners a piece of work made from their tree in payment.

You can also utilize offcuts from a sawmill provided that you approach the sawmill owner in the right way. You need to be able to persuade the owners that it is worth more for them to let you have the wood than to convert it into firewood, and this means that you must be prepared to pay something for it and not take up so much of the sawyer's time that you become a nuisance. You may even find that if you show them some examples of your work you might strike up a more productive relationship. You must be prepared to take some dross among the good stuff and this presupposes that you can

use the waste as firewood or can dispose of it in some other way.

SUITABLE WOODS

Be prepared to try anything, especially if it is free. But like all experimenters keep notes of what you have used and how you have used it, and be prepared to make mistakes. Avoid woods that have cracks and knots until you are thoroughly competent.

I have always used locally grown timber because, when I started turning, I could not afford imported wood. I grew to love native woods, which I now prefer in aesthetic and practical terms to any others.

When I became aware that timber grown in tropical areas is almost always felled and

extracted at the expense of irreversible damage to the fragile soil structure I gained another reason to prefer home-produced timber. In temperate zones it is possible to harvest timber without ruining the soil structure which means that it is relatively easy to renew the habitat. Indeed without the financial gain that landowners achieve from harvesting the timber many stands of trees would disappear from the landscape permanently.

Unfortunately, not using tropical hardwoods, and suggesting that others follow suit, does not do anything positive about the situation because the rainforests are not being felled just to harvest the timber. In many cases the money earned from the sale of the timber is only a side benefit of felling forests to free land on which people need to live and grow crops. If the timber cannot be sold it is either used for fuel or simply burned *in situ*.

Tropical timber can be harvested in an environmentally-friendly way by taking out selected trees which can regenerate and by transporting them by means that do not churn up the soil. The only timber importers that I know of who can provide evidence that has satisfied the Environmental watchdogs that their timber comes from such sources are listed in Useful Addresses. Responsible suppliers only sell tropical timber imported from countries where they have established that it is harvested by the local communities who know which trees to fell to maintain the forests and how to deal with the felled timber in such a way that the soil structure is not degraded. They try to ensure that it is in the interests of the locals to fell the timber in this way by paying them a good price. If the locals do not get a fair price they often sell out to a multi-national concern who proceed to clear-fell the area.

It is not possible for an individual to check whether his or her tropical timber comes from such a source and it is apparent that there are timber merchants whose claims to sell sustainable timber do not withstand close examination. Accreditation by the 'Wildlife Fund for Nature' and 'Friends of the Earth' is more reliable and if you support these charities you will be doing your bit to help sustain the source of the timber you are using.

The only way to be absolutely sure that the timber you use has not been harvested in a way that harms the environment is only to use wood that has been felled by storms or has outlived its usefulness in a garden, and there are many turners who can, and do, rely on these sources.

If you are unable to obtain timber from these sources then I suggest you approach your local sawmill. In my own area there are two that I use regularly (see Useful Addresses, p. 108) who have customers all over Britain, but if you make enquires in your own area you will no doubt be able to find some near you.

Among the woods that grow in temperate zones and are particularly good for turning are ash, elm, oak, sweet chestnut, sycamore (maple), London plane, wild cherry, yew, robinia, boxwood, and all the fruit woods. See individual sections on pp. 51 and 74 for notes on the best woods for spindle and bowl turning respectively.

If you are aware that your raw material comes from a tree, and has a structure that is intimately bound up with its function in that tree, then you will naturally turn it in a way that is sympathetic to its characteristics. This is one of the most important tenets of turning, but I believe it is equally important to be aware that what you are using as your raw material came from another living being whose existence is intimately bound up with yours.

—PART TWO ————————————

TECHNIQUES

−6

SPINDLE TURNING – MATERIALS

Spindle turning is done between centres, usually with the grain of the wood running parallel to the axis of rotation, as opposed to faceplate turning where the grain usually runs at right angles to the axis of rotation. The grain direction determines the method of working, and to a large extent, the tools used.

The commonest articles made in this way are chair legs and balusters (for stairs), but a vast number of items, can be made between centres, usually useful articles. If you examine them closely you will observe that they almost invariably have the grain running along the axis of the piece – this is because wood is strongest along the grain.

A chair exerts downward thrust on the legs and if the material they are made of has a tendency to shear at right angles to its axis, the legs would break. The longitudinal alignment of the grain is best for the turner because the wood has less of a tendency to break under the pressure exerted by the centres and because wood is easier to work along the grain. It is possible to turn wood between centres with the grain running at right angles to the axis, but it is not easy and not recommended for the inexperienced.

Because work produced between centres tends to be utilitarian and can usually be produced by copy lathes it tends to be more price-sensitive than other turning. This has lead to the idea that the spindle turner is an inferior beast to the bowl turner. This is an idea that should be discouraged because in fact the spindle turner needs to be more skilful than the bowl turner simply to compete. The artistic content of a piece of spindle work may be subservient to the functional, and the fact that it is very often repeated almost exactly may reduce its impact, but it is just as important as in bowl turning and it is harder to achieve an original and aesthetically satisfying result.

SUITABLE WOOD

For practice and repetition work the timber should be straight grained and free of knots. This is to make it easier for the turner and to make it stronger. To practice a new technique nothing beats using an unseasoned branch of whatever you can pick up for nothing, because it is free, easier to turn when wet and is already rounded. The bark tends to catch on the edge of the tool so it is a good idea to remove the bark with a knife before you start to turn.

If you do not have access to bits of tree you can often find bits of chair in skips and dumps, or perhaps you can raid the off-cut pile of your local timber merchant for odd, short lengths of anything that is going. Softwoods are quite good to practise on because you can make an impression on them without too much effort, but do be warned that to produce a good

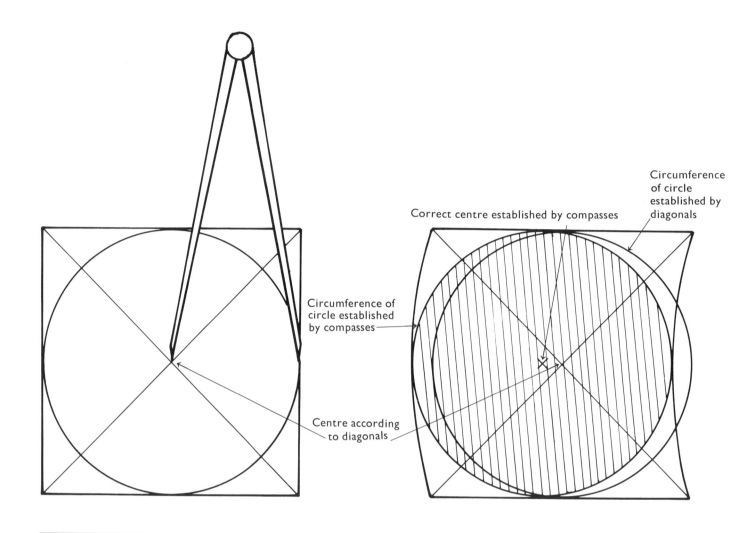

Fig. 39
Marking centre of spindle blank

finish straight from the tool requires better technique and sharper tools than with hardwoods. Softwoods usually produce an inferior product to hardwoods because they tend to be softer and therefore prone to damage.

Sycamore is one of the easiest woods to turn and is particularly useful for domestic kitchenware, such as rolling pins, steak bashers, honey dippers, raised pie moulds and tea caddies, because it is odourless and responds well to being washed in hot water. Ash is almost as easy to turn and often looks more attractive than sycamore, though the grain is a bit coarser. It is often used where its elasticity is an advantage such as in chair legs, but oak, elm (not so common now since the outbreak of Dutch Elm Disease), cherry, sweet chestnut and yew are also used for this purpose, and for many other items.

It is more important to make sure that the grain is straight and free of defects in spindle turning than to follow slavishly any recommendations as to species.

PREPARING THE WOOD

If you have never turned before I suggest that you start with a piece of wood about 150mm (6in) long and not more than 50mm (2in) thick. If it is already cylindrical, as in the case of a branch or perhaps an old chair leg or piece of broom handle, you will not have the problem of getting rid of the rough edges before you practise your gouge work.

First you must put in the driving centre and then move the tailstock so that the dead centre is about 150mm (6in) from the point of the driving centre. To fit the wood on to the lathe you have to establish the centre of each end. In the case of a square-section piece this is done by drawing diagonal lines on the end which naturally cross at the centre, but if you have a cylinder then you cannot do this and will have to use the method below. I use this as a matter of routine because I have found that quite often supposedly square-section stock is not actually square and diagonals do not always meet at the exact centre. I often use wood that I have dried after cutting

roughly square, and in this case the sides are often bowed which the diagonal method does not cater for; another good reason to use my method which with practice will become quicker than drawing diagonals.

First measure the diameter and then set a pair of compasses to half of that (the radius). Put one compass point where you think the centre is and swing the other point around to see if your guess was roughly correct. With practice you will find that your first guess is usually right, but if not, then try another place until you do get it right (fig. 39). You can then push the compass point into the wood so that it leaves a clear mark.

To ensure that the driving centre grips the wood you must make holes in the end for the fork to fit it. It is kindest to your bearings to do this by having a spare driving centre and driving it into the end with a mallet, but if you have robust bearings you can offer the wood up to the centre so that the centre point

engages and then hit the other end with a mallet; or line the wood up between the centres and tighten up the tailstock to force the forks into the wood. You must then unwind the tailstock a fraction so that there is not too much pressure on the bearings.

With the wood held firmly between centres you must check that the lathe is set at the correct speed. When you are trying a new technique it is better for this to be on the slow side so that you feel safe. Whereas a professional would probably turn a 50mm (2in) diameter piece at about 2000 rpm it would be safer for a novice to start at 500 rpm and speed up to a more efficient speed as confidence increases.

Next the rest must be put in place. It should be as close to the wood as possible, say a millimetre away and level with or slightly higher than the centre of the work. Always rotate the wood by hand before starting the lathe so that the wood does not snag against anything when you do start it up.

−7−

SPINDLE TURNING − TOOL TECHNIQUES

HANDS

In the following descriptions of the use of tools I will not say which hand should hold which end of the tool. This is because in turning there is no need to use one hand, say at the rest, in preference to the other. Both hands are of equal importance and neither hand is required to use much power or more skill. If you try changing the hands over at regular intervals while you are learning you will be able to use which hand is most convenient for any particular cut and it should prevent you from developing the sort of condition in your tendons (such as tennis elbow) that comes with repeating actions too frequently.

Even if you have been turning for a long time and consistently using either the right hand or the left hand at the rest, I strongly recommend that you try to reverse hands from time to time, if only because it makes you analyze exactly what both hands

do – this may lead to unexpected refinements of technique, as it did for me.

How you hold the tool at the rest is largely a matter of personal preference. As you may see from the photos I have a somewhat unusual style which stems from having learned to move each finger separately while playing musical instruments. It is more usual and perhaps easier to put the heel of the hand on the rest and all the fingers on the tool with the thumb under the rest (**fig. 40**) or put the fingers under the rest and the thumb on the tool (**fig. 41**). The only golden rule is never to allow your fingers to go between the work and the rest, which can be very painful.

POSITIONING TOOLS

If you think about woodturning in the simplest of terms, i.e. holding a sharp edge against a fast rotating piece of wood, it is

quite remarkable that catches do not occur all the time. What prevents it is the way that the edge is ground and the angle at which the tool is held. These factors combine to make the edge cut off a thin shaving rather than plunge into the wood.

It is easy to think of turning in isolation from other types of woodwork but going back to basics can teach us much about the use of tools. If you consider the ordinary carpenter's chisel, it is not the fact that the wood is stationary that prevents the chisel from digging in, but the angle at which the tool is held relative to the work. Do not take my word for it; try a planing cut with a chisel and you will see that if you hold the tool so that the bevel is rubbing it will produce a clean cut, whereas if you hold it at a steeper angle it will dig in.

With all turning tools it is safest to try the tool against the work before you start the lathe and work out at what angle the bevel will prevent a dig in. Then

Fig. 40
Position of hand on rest, thumb under

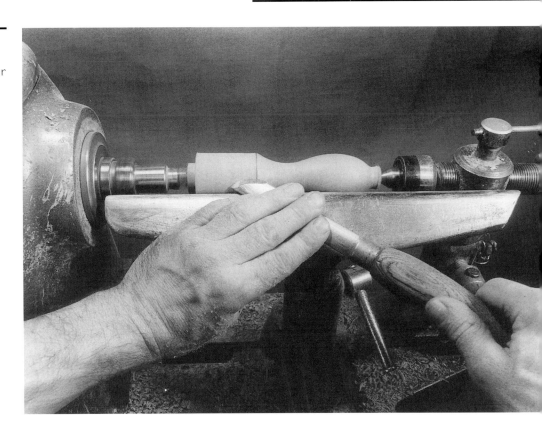

Fig. 41
Position of hand on rest, thumb over

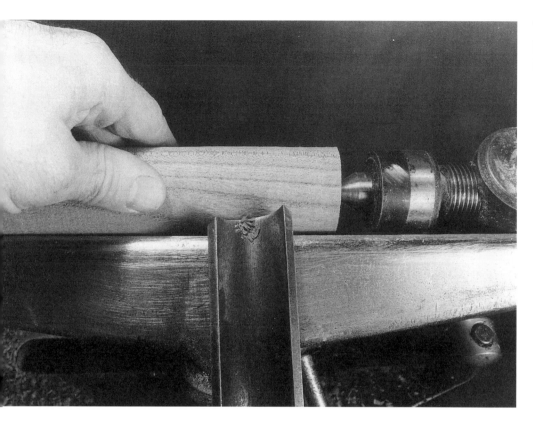

Fig. 42
Rotating wood by hand, gouge at 90°

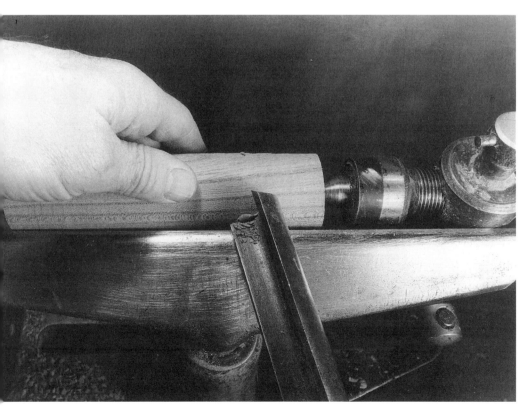

Fig. 43
Rotating wood by hand, gouge at 70°

you can rotate the wood by hand and only when you are really happy need you start the lathe. See Chapter Four for details of all tools referred to in Part Two.

ROUGHING GOUGE

This is the tool that is used to convert the stock quickly to a centred cylinder, whether it be from a cylinder which has been centred innacurately or a square-section blank. Assuming that you are starting with a cylinder of wood, before you start the lathe try to work out how to hold the tool so that the bevel and the edge rub against the circumference of the cylinder at the same time. This is easy to do if the rest is at centre height and the tool is pointing upwards and at right angles to the axis of the lathe (**fig. 42 and fig. 7, p. 31**).

When you roll the tool by rotating your wrist you will see that the bevel and edge will rub in the same way at any given point along the whole of the length of the edge while the tool is at right angles. Even if you hold the tool so that it is at an angle of about 70° to the axis you can still rub the bevel and edge because the bevel is concave and the circumference of the cylinder is naturally circular (**fig. 43 and fig. 7, p. 31**).

As you will see from **fig. 42**, if you rotate the wood towards yourself by hand when the gouge is at right angles to the axis, you will cut a groove in the wood on

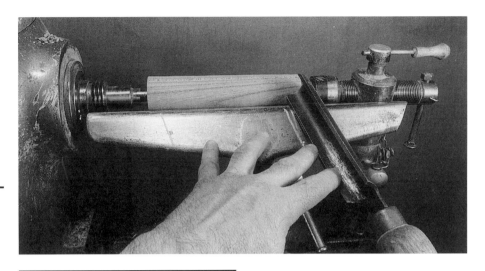

Fig. 44
Lines on rest

one circumference, but if you move the tool handle slightly to the right while keeping the cutting edge at the same position on the wood, you should feel the tool pulled towards the left. This is what you want to happen when you are using any gouge, and it is an important practical exposition of the fact that if you present the tool to the work at the correct angle you do not have to push it to make it cut.

As long as some part of the bevel and the edge of the tool are in contact with the wood, the tool is supported and you should not get a dig in. Experimenting with the tool before starting to turn will show you that there is a range of positions where this important principle is satisfied.

The action of roughing out with this gouge is to start with the tool at one end of the work with the tool rolled over on its side, so that the part of the edge

in contact with the work is part way between the middle and the end. Be careful not to allow the very end of the edge to make contact with the wood as this will catch. If you are starting at the right end of the work the hollow of the gouge should be pointing to the left.

When you have established the angle at which the tool cuts, you must keep the tool at this angle while it traverses the length of the wood. This will become second nature to you with practice, but to make sure that you achieve this, put a line on the rest at the right-hand end at the angle you have established using chalk or wax crayon, and then draw a line at the same angle (i.e. parallel to the first line) on the left-hand end (**fig. 44**). Practise sliding the tool across the rest maintaining the angle and you may find that it is quite difficult to achieve.

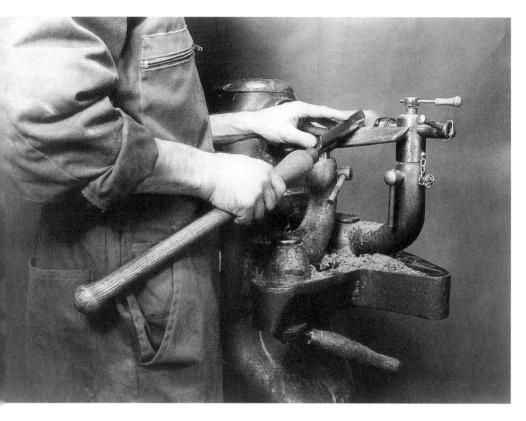

Fig. 45
Tool handle supported by body, right end of cut

The way most experienced turners manage it is to hold the tool so that one hand is on the rest, holding the tool against it, and the other hand is at the end of the handle, but supported by the hip or whichever part of the body is at the appropriate height **(fig. 45)**. To cut from right to left start with the weight on your right foot and gradually transfer it to the left foot as the cut progresses. With your whole body supporting the tool it is easier to keep it steady. If you wish to alter the angle of the tool slightly you do it by rolling the bottom hand and moving the position of the tool on the rest with the other hand. If you examine **figs. 45–46** you will see that the operator has changed position, but this was achieved without moving the feet and the tool has changed its position simply by rotating the wrist.

When you are happy with the method of cutting from right to left, you can try to work out how to cut from left to right, which of course is to roll the tool over so that the part in contact with the wood is between the right-hand end and the centre of the edge. The angle of the tool should also change over so that it leans into the cut from the left, and the whole action is reversed so that the weight of the supporting body is transferred from the left foot to the right. When you become proficient at the cut you will be able to go up and down the wood in one flowing movement. Now you have practised what you need to do with the wood still or only hand-powered you are ready to try it powered by lathe.

After some practice with the roughing gouge you should eventually reduce the piece of wood you started with to little more than a toothpick. For your

Fig. 46
Change in positions at left hand of cut

next exercise I suggest you start with a piece of square-section softwood of similar dimensions to the first piece. Perhaps it is a bit daunting at this stage to think of roughing from the square to the round so you can help yourself by removing the corners while the wood is between centres, but stationary, by using a plane or drawknife.

This piece will be rougher than the cylinder you tried first but when you start up the lathe you will notice that the edges of the wood are blurred and as in all cases where you start with non-

circular edges you must address the tool to the work as though the outer, blurred, edge is the one you are turning, which of course it is. In **fig. 47** overleaf you can see the cut from right to left and in **fig. 48** you can see from left to right. Practise using the roughing gouge as before until you are left with another rough toothpick.

You may now feel that you are confident enough to rough out from a piece of square-section stock. It would be a good idea to start with a piece that is just 25mm (1in) square so that it is not quite so terrifying, but do

remember to turn the wood by hand before you start the lathe to ensure that it can rotate without touching the rest.

The roughing gouge is used to reduce rough stock to the cylindrical and can easily produce the quality of finish seen in **fig. 49**, but it can also be used to do preliminary shaping. Just by exerting a bit more pressure at one point on the wood you can produce a shallow cove and this is good practice. In fact, you will find it a lot easier to make a succession of shallow coves than a straight cylinder.

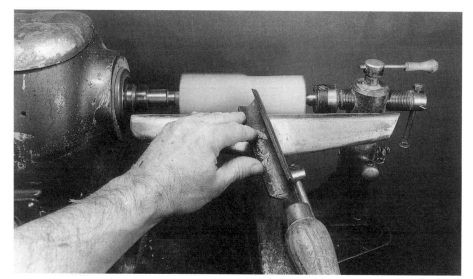

Fig. 47
Roughing gouge, cutting right to left

Fig. 48
Roughing gouge, cutting left to right

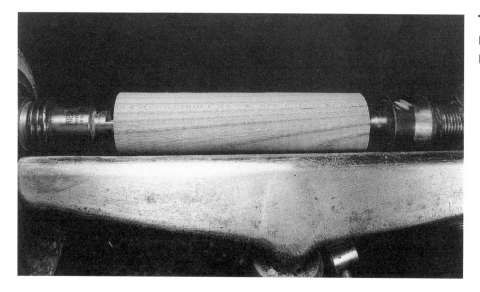

Fig. 49
Finish from roughing gouge

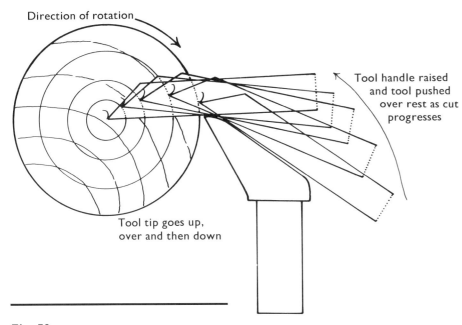

Direction of rotation

Tool handle raised
and tool pushed
over rest as cut
progresses

Tool tip goes up,
over and then down

Fig. 50
Fluted parting tool, arc of cut

BEADING AND PARTING CHISEL

I use this tool particularly for removing a lot of wood quickly where a deep narrow groove is required. It does not leave a very smooth-sided cut but the side can always be finished off using a skew. The bottom of the cut can be made smooth with the beading tool using light cuts.

I tend to use roughing gouges and beading tools for heavy cuts and keep the skew for fine cuts because the heavy cuts soon blunt the tool and I like to keep my skews sharp.

If you try the beading chisel before starting the lathe you will see that in order to make the bevel support the edge, the tool must be pointed upwards. In fact, the cut is started with the edge being supported by the bevel as much as possible and then as the cut progresses the chisel is pushed over the rest, in the same manner as the fluted parting tool in **fig. 50**, otherwise the bevel would lose contact, the edge would no longer be fully under control, and would soon become blunt. This chisel is used at right angles to the axis for this cut, and I used it at the left end of the piece of wood that I used in the photos in this section before forming the beads, so that my tools did not foul the driving centre (**fig. 51**).

Fig. 51
Beading and parting chisel

FLUTED PARTING TOOL
(see fig. 18, p. 36)

The fluted parting tool is useful for making very narrow deep grooves (as when parting off) and produces a smooth-sided cut with a convex bottom. It is used with the flute downwards and in the same way as the beading chisel, i.e. with an up and over action, so that at the bottom of the cut the tool overhangs more than at the start. I have shown this cut in **fig. 50** and as already mentioned the same arc is described by the beading and parting tool and the skew (p. 68) when doing the slicing cut. This tool can also be used to take a cut off the end of a spindle to stop the other tools fouling the centre **(figs. 52–53)**. It has been criticized for scoring the tool rest but I think for certain jobs its special characteristics are so worthwhile that I am willing to spend a few moments filing the rest every so often.

SPINDLE GOUGE

Comparing **fig. 54** with **fig. 20** in Chapter Four, you will see the main differences between the roughing gouge and the spindle gouge are that in the latter the flute is more shallow, and the nose is ground with the bevel curved back along the side instead of at a right angle. On the rare occasions that I use a spindle gouge I use the carving gouge that you see in **fig. 54**. You could use a narrow bowl gouge for the

Fig. 52
Fluted parting tool, start of cut

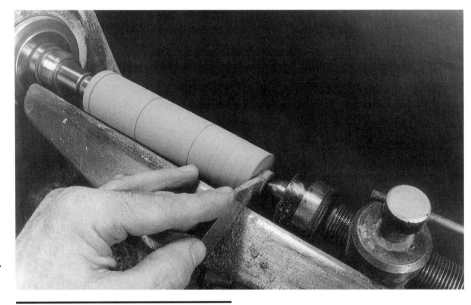

Fig. 53
Fluted parting tool, end of cut

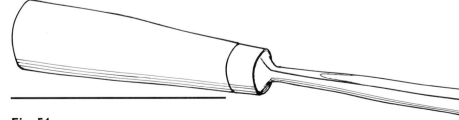

Fig. 54
Spindle gouge 12.5mm ($\frac{1}{2}$in)

Fig. 55
Spindle gouge, right side of cove

Fig. 56
Spindle gouge, left side of cove

same purpose but it is a bit of a waste because you do not require all the strength that that tool possesses for spindle work.

The method described in the previous section for working out the correct angle at which to use the roughing gouge also applies to this and any other gouge. So if you try out this tool with the work stationary you will be able to discover at what angles you need to hold it so that the bevel supports the edge.

As an exercise, take a piece of square-section stock about 15 × 50 × 50mm (6 × 2 × 2in) and reduce it to a cylinder using the roughing gouge. While the wood is revolving put two pencil lines 50mm (2in) apart to mark the edges of a cove. To cut a cove, start at one side and cut towards the middle, then go to the other side and do likewise **(figs. 55– 56)**. This is because, as you will remember from Chapter Five and the analogy of the bundle of straws, wood with the grain running lengthwise does not respond well to being cut uphill because the fibres you are cutting are not supported by any other fibres.

Hold the gouge on its side pointing upward so that you are cutting in the top quarter of the wood. The part of the edge in contact with the wood should be halfway between the left end and the nose when you are cutting the right side of the cove, and vice versa for the left side. As the cove deepens and you get to the centre of the cove the gouge should be rolled as though you

Fig. 57
Spindle gouge, centre of cove

were scooping ice cream (**fig. 57**), but at the end of the cut in the centre of the cove you should still not be cutting with the nose of the gouge.

You may well wonder why, since the tool is rounded like the cove, you cannot just push the tool horizontally at the wood. You can try it if you like, but do it at a very slow speed for you are bound to get a catch, because it is impossible to have the edge supported by the bevel along its entire length. You can only cut with one part of an edge at once.

As the cove deepens you will find that the gouge has to be held more horizontally to keep the bevel rubbing. In order to make the bottom of the cove smooth you must feather the cut as you get there so that you are cutting the very thinnest of shavings when you lift off the gouge. You should eventually be able to

make a 25mm (1in) wide cove with a 12mm (½in) gouge, so a 50mm (2in) cove should be no trouble to start with.

As the cove gets deeper you may well find that you get a catch at the top of the cut. This is because by then there will be a sharp shoulder where the original surface of the cylinder meets the cove, and there is no way you can rub the bevel as you start the cut. There is no problem if you want a rounded edge to the shoulder because you can roll the tool over keeping the bevel rubbing as you go, but if you want a sharp-edged shoulder all you can do is remember the angle at which the bevel will rub when you are further down the cove, and start gently but firmly with the tool at this angle at the top of the slope.

There are two sure ways to get a catch: one is to dither and the

other is to be too abrupt! But if you make no mistake you should be able use the gouge to achieve a finish at least as good as in **fig. 58**.

Making beads with the spindle gouge is easy once you have mastered coves, as it requires a similar rolling movement using the same area of the edge. As with coves you work from the apex of the bead downhill on one side and then do the other. **Figs. 59–62** show a gentle bead that would be a good shape to start with and requires no great skill to develop into a steep bead. **Fig. 63** shows the finish you should be able to achieve from the tool.

Most people find the gouge is the easiest tool to use for spindle turning and it can do most shapes you are likely to require except sharp changes of direction and deep, narrow grooves, which is where the chisels come in.

Fig. 58
Spindle gouge, finish

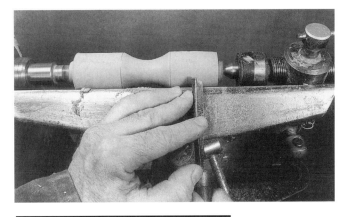

Fig. 59
Spindle gouge, right side of bead

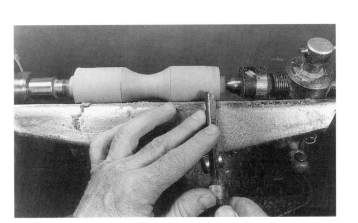

Fig. 60
Spindle gouge, right side of bead

Fig. 61
Spindle gouge, left side of bead

Fig. 62
Spindle gouge, left side of bead

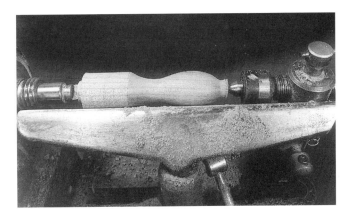

Fig. 63
Spindle gouge, finish from tool

SKEW CHISEL
(see fig. 13, p. 35)

The skew is the most versatile spindle tool and when you have got the hang of it you can do everything you need except the narrowest of coves and grooves. There is no other tool that can make such a smooth cut but it can take a long time to learn to get it right. If you do make the effort you will be entitled to feel pleased with yourself for it is the most satisfying tool to use.

Skews are supplied with a straight edge and whereas these work all right, they are easier and more versatile if you sharpen them to a curved edge as I explain in Chapter Four. This is not a new idea of mine but was the traditional shape used by German turners.

When discussing the skew I shall refer to the sharp end as the point or toe and the other end of the edge as the heel. If you are lucky enough to discover an old skew chisel you may well find that at the heel end it has had the hard shoulder between the bevel and the tool surface ground back. This is because when turning coves, this shoulder rubs against the surface and can leave a groove. This problem is eradicated in the new generation of skew chisels made from oval-section steel and this pattern has the additional benefit of facilitating the rolling action that in the old type was more difficult to achieve smoothly because of the square edges. If you already have a skew made from square-

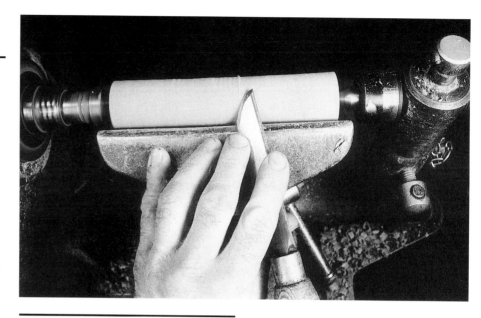

Fig. 64
Skew, point up, planing cut

section steel it is not too difficult to round off the edges with the grinder.

There are three basic cuts that the skew can make: planing, peeling and slicing.

Planing cut

This is the commonest cut and can be used to convert square stock to a smooth cylinder. I prefer to use a roughing gouge to remove the square edges so that I keep the skew sharp, but if I am turning a small diameter piece I use a skew for the whole operation.

Again I would recommend that you practise on a piece 150 × 50 × 50mm (6 × 2 × 2in). Before you start, position the tool rest as close to the work as possible and rotate the wood by

hand to ensure that it does not snag. The rest should be about the same height as the centre.

Take off the edges of the wood with the roughing gouge and then stop the lathe to work out at what angles the skew will cut while properly supported by the bevel.

As you may well discover, the number of different ways you can hold the skew so that the edge is in contact and the bevel supporting it are numerous. The traditional way of doing this for the planing cut is with the point up and using a part of the edge part way between the point and heel. The angle the skew subtends with the work depends on the angle of the skew edge, the angle of the bevel and the cutting characteristics of the wood; but if the angle at the point of the skew between the straight edge and the bevel is about 40°, the straight side of the tool should be about 10° off the right angle to the axis. These are not exact angles to be followed slavishly but they may give you an idea of where to start (fig. 64). In all fairness to traditional skew users, the skew I am using in this photo has been ground specifically for use in the 'toe down' position, and a 'normal' skew, which has the angle between the straight side and the bevel of 60 to 70°, can be presented to the work at about 30° off the right angle when cutting 'toe up' and cuts very effectively.

When you have worked out the angle, you must use the skew rather as you did the roughing gouge, in so far as you need to slide it along the rest all the way at the same angle, so if you find this hard, draw two lines on the rest as I suggested in the roughing gouge passage.

Remember to think through what you are going to do before you do it, which means that you start off a cut from right to left with the weight on your right foot, and gradually transfer it to your left foot. This cut demands fine control because if you do not get the angles and the amount of pressure just right you will get a rough cut or a catch. You cannot allow your traverse of the work to be interrupted by any scars on the rest, so file them off before you start.

Because the angles are so critical you must make minute adjustments all the time which depend on your sensitivity to what the wood is telling you. You cannot develop this rapport overnight but you ought to be open to the possibility of it, which means that you must not grip the tool so that your knuckles turn white. I know you may well be expecting a catch any moment, but I can assure you that since you are bound to suffer this anyway and even the tightest grip will not prevent it, you might as well relax. In fact, if you are hanging on to the tool for dear life when the catch occurs you will do more damage than if your grip allows the tool to have its evil way. The main point of practising techniques before you try to make anything is to make mistakes without ruining a project.

The reasons for catches are variations on a simple theme: either you force the tool to do more than it can so the edge loses the support of the bevel, or you are too tentative and make a dithering dab at the wood at a wrong angle. If you are wearing the right safety gear and are not turning a large piece at too fast a speed catches will do you no harm, but you must stop and analyze what went wrong so that you can reduce the frequency of it happening again.

Sometimes as you keep trying at a technique and keep making the same mistake, you get tenser and your muscles are less controllable. When you get to this stage for goodness sake stop and do something else or you might end up giving up turning for good.

I very rarely do the planing cut with the point up because it is so much easier with the point down. You can present the edge at the same angle to the work this way and the great advantage is that as you move the skew across the work the tool is held so that your forearm and the tool are in a straight line and working at an angle only 45° or so off the direction of cut (fig. 65). You can see in fig. 66 overleaf that the part of the edge doing the cutting is just beyond the toe. The hand on the rest has little work to do which means that it is free to leave the rest and support the work should it flex or be in the process of parting off. With the point up, the whole tool subtends a greater angle with the direction of cut and requires more steadying from the hand on the rest. It feels awkward in comparison.

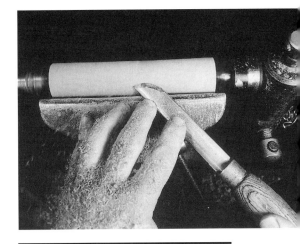

Fig. 65
Skew, point down, planing cut

67

Fig. 66

Skew, point down, planing cut, close up

With the edge of the skew ground in a curve you have a greater variety of angles available at which to present the tool to the work, and if you find that the grain does not cut cleanly with the point down you can change the angle so that the edge is practically parallel to the axis. This only works if the edge is curved, because then only a small part of the edge is in contact with the work. However, it does not produce such a clean cut as the proper planing cut because the bevel ridge does not follow the cutting edge. The edge is only supported by a part of the bevel, and because you are cutting across the grain you will not produce the fine shavings which are always such a good indicator of a clean cut.

If the grain is unruly and you cannot produce a fine cut it is always a good idea to apply some liquid to the wood to make the fibres cut more easily. This can be either oil or water – whichever is compatible with your preferred finish. On those occasions when you may not be able to get a clean cut with the skew, you may succeed with a gouge instead.

You should always aim to get a good finish from the tool because excessive sanding tends to alter the sharp edges produced by the tool, renders the work less round, and produces more health-damaging dust.

Peeling cut

Sometimes you need to remove a large quantity of wood from the end of a cylinder, for example when forming a spigot. You can use a beading and parting chisel to do this or you can use a skew – the principle is the same. The tool is held so that the edge is parallel to the axis, its widest face flat on the rest **(fig. 67)**. You will not be able to take a very wide cut because it will exert more force on the work than the driving centre can impart, which means that it will drill a hole in the end. Aim to take a cut 3mm ($\frac{1}{8}$in) wide, rest the bevel on the work, raise the handle end and push upwards into the work. The progress of the edge from outside to centre describes an arc when viewed from the end **(see fig. 50, p. 61)**.

Slicing cut

The slicing cut is the one to use to form beads and coves which, as I have already described, can be done with a gouge – but I always do it with the skew. This cut describes the same arc as the peeling cut but uses the point of the skew to clean off the end of the piece. The contact between the tool and the rest is on the narrow face of the tool, and the bevel rubs behind the point so that the tool subtends an angle to the axis exactly equal to the bevel **(fig. 68)**. If you get this wrong a catch results, but when you get it right no sanding is necessary.

You can use the heel for this cut but this is very much more difficult, as you will see if you try it, because the point you are using is obscured by the rest of the tool.

If you start off with the usual 150mm × 50 × 50mm (6 × 2 × 2in) square-section blank and take off the edges with the roughing gouge you can mark off the centre 50mm portion with pencil lines and make this into a cove. Either side of this is space for two beads. You will not be able to do the central faces of the beads until you have done the cove but you can do the outer faces, and since this is an easier cut than for a cove I shall describe it first.

It is usually the case in spindle turning that you need to get rid of the ends of the blank because of the marks left by the centres. When you are practising it is a good idea to make a groove in the ends so that you do not allow the tool to slip on to the dead or driving centre, which always results in a trip to the grinder. You can do this by making

Fig. 67
Skew, peeling cut

Fig. 68
Skew, slicing cut

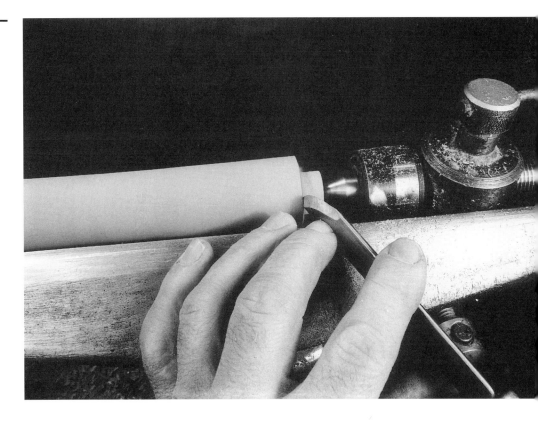

Fig. 69
Skew, right side of bead

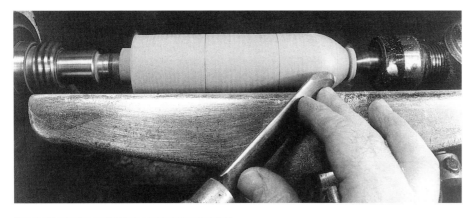

Fig. 70
Skew, right side of bead, rounding

Fig. 71
Skew, right side of bead

grooves about 12.5mm ($\frac{1}{2}$in) from both ends with the fluted parting tool. Make sure that you leave enough wood in the centre at least as thick as the fork centre to support the work.

This will leave you with a sharp shoulder where the rounded curve of one side of the bead should be, and you can convert this by using a variation of the slicing cut. For the right-hand bead enter the wood at the point of the shoulder with the point of the skew **(fig. 69)**. The end of the tool handle should be over to your left and you should take off small amounts to make a 45° slope until you reach the point where the outside of the potential bead is in sight **(fig. 70)**.

Then start at the top of the slope, but instead of going straight down, roll the wrists over to make the sides curved **(figs. 70–71)**. As you progress with the cut you should use part of the edge beyond the point as this gives a smoother finish. Never try to take off too much too quickly as you will have a catch.

Since you are going to make two beads on the one piece of wood it is good practice to try to make them equal. This is best done by standing so that your head is equidistant between the beads and making the right bead with your right hand on the rest, and the left bead with your left hand on the rest. It is important to keep your head still when copying a shape because if you view a shape with your head in one position and then move it when you are trying to replicate the shape, you will find that it is difficult to get a precise copy because your perception of the shape of a curve alters with the angle you are viewing it from. This is known as the parallex error **(figs. 72–73)**.

The cove in the middle should also be done with your head directly over the cove to eliminate parallex error, but since both sides of the cove are so near to each other you do not need to change over hands.

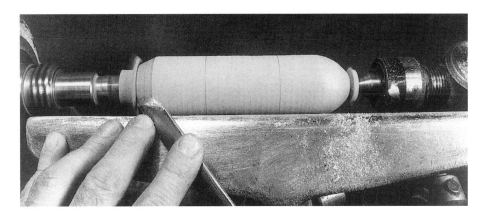

Fig. 72
Skew, left side of bead

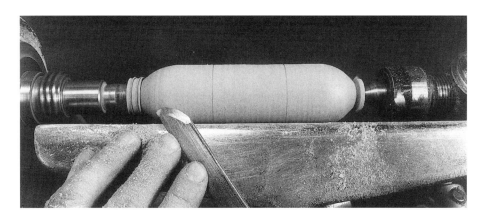

Fig. 73
Skew, left side of bead

Fig. 74
Skew, cove, starting

Start the cove by making a 'V' cut in the middle, by entering the wood with the point and cutting first one side and then the other following the angle of the bevel; this means that when you cut the left side of the 'V', the end of the handle should be over to the left **(fig. 74)** and when you cut the right side it should be over to the right. If this is not so, your bevel will not be rubbing and you will get a catch. One advantage of skews having short handles is that you can pass the tool between your body and the work

when you are doing a cove like this.

As the 'V' is deepened and widened **(figs. 75–76)** you will find it easier to cut with the part of the edge just behind the point, and you will have to raise the handle so that the point of the skew reaches down into the bottom. When you have almost reached the depth and curvature that you want, the action of the skew has to change so that the sides can be curved **(figs. 77–79)**. **Fig. 80** shows the finish you can achieve with the skew.

This requires a rolling action rather like that used with the spindle gouge. If you make a very deep and narrow cove with the skew, you will find that at the very bottom the end of the tool handle is in the air, with the toe below the level of the rest. At this stage you have no bevel rubbing at all and you must be particularly careful.

With all these techniques at your command you should be able to tackle most spindle projects. For advice on finishing, see Chapter Ten.

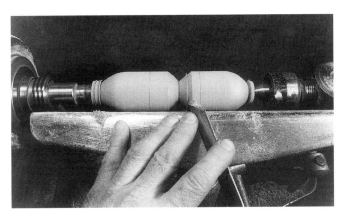

Fig. 75
Skew, cove, deepening and widening

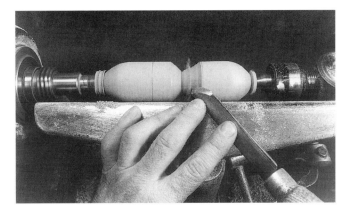

Fig. 76
Skew, cove, deepening and widening

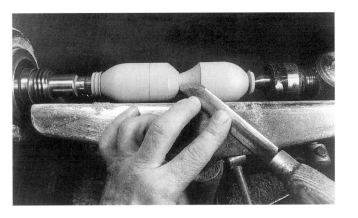

Fig. 77
Skew, cove, rounding right side

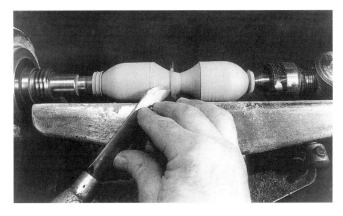

Fig. 78
Skew, cove, rounding left side

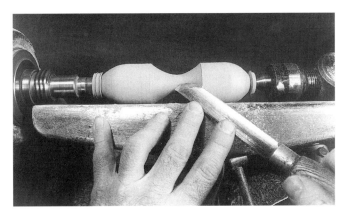

Fig. 79
Skew, cove, rounding centre

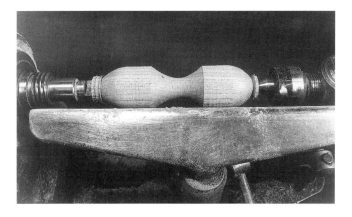

Fig. 80
Skew, cove, finish from tool

−8−

FACEPLATE TURNING – MATERIALS & SETTING UP

In the next two chapters I will cover the tool techniques needed to make such objects as bowls, platters, and breadboards, which usually have the grain of the wood running across them. In other words they are turned with the grain running at right angles to the axis of the lathe. This means that you encounter the end grain at least twice per revolution on the circumference, in contrast to spindles where the end grain is only present at the ends. This demands different cutting techniques.

SUITABLE WOOD

It is not so easy to economize on timber for practice purposes in faceplate turning because the blanks are necessarily larger than in the case of spindle turning. However, if you can obtain wet wood you will find that it is cheaper and easier to practise on than seasoned wood.

The most suitable woods for utilitarian ware are sycamore (or maple), ash (as in the photos) and the fruit woods. All these are good for the less experienced turner because they present no particular difficulties, unlike burrs and the more wildly grained woods that ought not to be used until a fairly high level of skill is achieved.

PREPARING THE WOOD

I suggest that you try unfamiliar techniques on the cheapest wood that you can lay your hands on, and expect to waste it, rather than struggle to produce a finished object while you are still worried about making a mistake. But do not try to economize by using wood with a lot of shakes, because this can be hazardous.

Try to obtain some wet sycamore or fruitwood in a 50mm (2in) to 75mm (3in) thick plank and mark a 20cm (8in) circle with

dividers. Make sure that you mark the centre at the same time so that you can easily locate the centre when you come to fit the faceplate. Cut the circle as accurately as you can to make it easy to turn.

METHODS OF SUPPORT

This type of turning can be loosely described as faceplate turning, but it is useful to remember that when the pole lathe was the only engine available for turning, all these items were made between centres and the marks left by the centres were removed when the object was parted from the lathe. Nests of bowls were commonly made this way and in old examples you can still see the marks in the middle of the bowls where the cleaning up was done.

There are now sophisticated methods available for holding blanks that seek to conceal all

Fig. 81
Bowl blank screwed to faceplate

traces of how the object was held. For the purposes of this book I shall not be going into these in detail because I am primarily concerned with basic techniques, but I would like to point out that there is no reason why you should go to great lengths to hide how you supported the object except for personal taste. Some of the best ceramic pots, which sell for sums of money rarely commanded by wood, show quite clearly how they were supported in the kiln and no one thinks amiss of this.

When you are just starting to turn it is better that you concern yourself with learning tool techniques rather than investing time and money on expensive chucks and possibly dangerous

techniques. Most lathes are supplied with at least one faceplate and this is all you need to start with.

The wood can be screwed to the faceplate or you can screw a disc of wood to it and stick the blank to it with glue. I have a recipe for glue I found in a book called *Every Man His Own Mechanic*, written in 1882, which says, 'Take of resin four parts and of pitch one part; set these ingredients by the fire to melt in an old pan or earthen pipkin, and when the mixture is liquid stir in sufficient finely powdered brick-dust to make it a stiff paste'. We are fortunate in having a wide selection of glues available nowadays so I have not tried it: I suggest you try PVA, thick

cyanoacrylate (super glue) or hot glue. If you put a sheet of paper between the wood and the disc it is easier to part them when you have finished.

I recommend that the beginner screws the wood directly to the faceplate because you can use as many and as strong screws as your competence demands. You will probably need four that project 19mm ($\frac{3}{4}$in) into the wood for your first efforts but eventually graduate to two that project only 12mm ($\frac{1}{2}$in) **(fig. 81)**.

If you mount the blank so that what will eventually be the bottom is facing outwards, you can shape and finish it and then reverse it for shaping the top. The base should be slightly concave so that it sits steadily,

Fig. 82
Precision combination chuck

but apart from this the design of the base can be as you like.

If in time you decide that you do not like screw holes in the base I suggest you use the glue method to do the final mounting, but if you can afford it, an expanding chuck **(fig. 82)** is a reasonably priced method of avoiding screw holes and the glue you need to fill them. Incidentally, you may notice that I have adapted the chuck by drilling extra holes in the body and ring so that I do not have to rotate it to find a suitable hole to alter the tension, and that I have also extended the 'C' spanners to give extra leverage and avoid

barking my knuckles on the bases of bowls.

My personal preference is against the recess left by an expanding chuck, as I prefer to design my own bottoms rather than have them dictated by the chuck manufacturer. I prefer to use the Axminster system which is based on a four-jaw, self-centring chuck, and which has a range of fitments that give you the options of an expanding chuck and wood-plate jaws. These enable you to remount the work for removing the recess when you have finished **(fig. 83)**. Of course this is more expensive than a simple faceplate and not to

be recommended until you are a thoroughly committed bowl turner.

The way I locate the faceplate on to the centre mark is to use a hardboard template made as follows: cut a piece of hardboard to the same size as the faceplate and then screw it on to the faceplate. Put it on the lathe, and when you start it up you will be able to see where the centre lies, because this is the only point where a pencil will produce a single dot rather than a circle. Then make a hole in the centre with a bradawl and take the faceplate off the lathe, removing the hardboard disc. If you put

Fig. 83
Axminster chuck with jaws, woodplates and dovetail jaws

the centre hole of the disc over the centre point of the blank, the holes from the screws that mounted the hardboard on the faceplate will enable you to mark where you need to make holes to mount the blank. If you mark them with the bradawl and then remove the hardboard, you can then make holes for the screws. You should be able to do this with the bradawl, but if you do not have strong enough wrists you may have to drill them, in which case you must make sure

that you avoid drilling too deep.

Do make sure that you screw the screws in very tightly and when you put the blank on the lathe wriggle it about before you start, to ensure that it is firm. If the screws are not tight the blank will work loose and that is best avoided. Another thing to check before you start the lathe is that the blank can rotate without touching the rest. Finally, check that the speed is correct, i.e. slow, for your first practice cuts, and then a little faster as you get

more confident.

You may well see the work of established turners in magazines and exhibitions where beautiful woods and sophisticated techniques have been used to great effect and be inspired to emulate them. This is good but I do suggest that before you try these timbers and techniques that you practice the basics first. The work you see in these high profile shop-windows has only been produced after much practice.

—9—
FACEPLATE TURNING – TOOL TECHNIQUES

All wood cutting techniques are influenced by the direction of the grain and if you study the blank in **(fig. 81)** you will see that the grain runs across the blank, i.e. at right angles to the axis of the lathe. This means that you should always cut so that the fibres you are cutting are supported by the fibres underneath. It is not as simple as saying that you should always cut downhill because it depends which way you are looking.

A secondary consideration is that as the wood rotates it tries to push anything in contact with it outwards from the centre, which is known as centrifugal force. It is easier to control your tool if you work against this force, i.e. towards the centre. That is why, in addition to grain direction, you should always hollow bowls from the outside in. If you hollow a bowl the other way it is very dangerous because if you lose control of the tool the force you are using plus centrifugal force will tend to make the tool dig into the side walls of the bowl.

On flat work or the outside of a bowl centrifugal force does not represent such a danger because if you work from the centre out and lose control it will tend to throw the tool clear of the work.''

TECHNIQUES FOR BOTH BOWLS AND FLATWARE

When making a bowl or piece of flatware it is not always necessary to make the blank perfectly circular by trueing up the edge and face, but it may be necessary in some circumstances, so here is how I do it. I start by making the face slightly concave using the 12.5mm ($\frac{1}{2}$in) gouge ground straight across **(see fig. 84)**. The tool passes from the edge towards the middle with the channel in the gouge (the flute) pointing in the direction of cut, as in **figs. 84–85**. In these photos I am holding the tool in two different ways with the right hand at the rest. I usually use a

variation of the fingers-on-top method and this has the advantage that you can use a spare finger or two to deflect the shavings from your face. Also, remember to try all techniques, alternating both hands at the rest to cut down stress due to repetition.

The part of the tool that does the cutting can be seen in the photos and is the part of the edge between the centre of the channel and the bottom end of the edge. Do not allow the end of the edge to come into contact with the work or it will dig in.

The edge should be supported by the bevel and the bottom end of the handle should be held against the hip to give it stability **(see fig. 45, p. 58)**. The movement should come from the transference of body weight from one foot to the other rather than from the arms.

Practise this movement with the lathe at rest to make sure that you can work out the angle at which the bevel will rub, so that the rest is set at the correct height

Fig. 84
Hand at rest, thumb over

Fig. 85
Hand at rest, thumb under

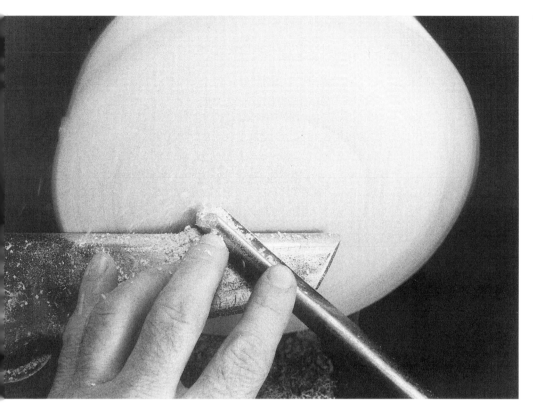

Fig. 86
Bowl gouge, ground-back, smoothing
cut

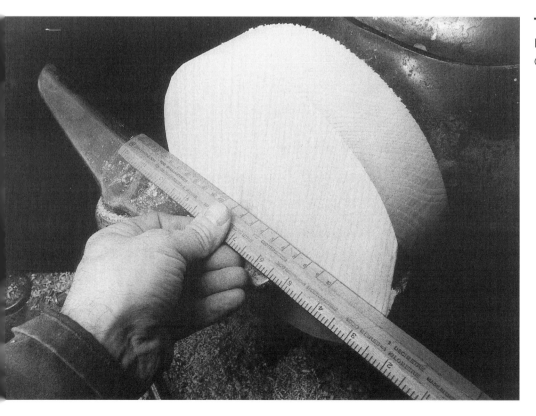

Fig. 87
Checking flatness of base

Fig. 88
Trueing edge

for your cut to end up exactly at the middle. This will vary with your height and the bevel angle, but it is important to get it right or you will have difficulty with the very middle of the cut, creating a peak there. If you need an easy way to reset the rest at the same height, you can put washers on the rest column or make a sleeve of the required thickness.

I like to turn the base roughly flat with the straight-across-gouge **(see fig. 24, p. 37)** cutting into the centre, and then, when the base is slightly concave, do a smoothing cut with the ground-back gouge **(see fig. 25, p. 37)** working outwards **(fig. 86)**.

Centrifugal force has little effect on this cut because the cut is done with the edge at right angles to the direction of rotation, so it does not matter whether you cut inwards or outwards. This cut is a fine one producing a good finish from a sharp tool, but it requires great care. If you allow the tool to rotate too far so that the edge is not supported by the bevel, a catch is certain. It is a simple matter to check the slight concavity of the base with a ruler **(fig. 87)**.

When you have finished the base you will need to do the side. If you are making a breadboard, for instance, and want the edge to be more or less at right angles to

the base, you must move the rest around so that it is parallel to the side. It is safest to do this when the lathe is at rest. This cut is quite difficult partly because the blank is not round. Also, because you start off with the tool beyond the work, the first part of the edge to come into contact with the work is not supported by the bevel. For these reasons, if you do not need to make the blank circular at this stage it is better to turn the outside working from the face (see below).

If you do need to true the side I suggest you use the ground-back gouge **(fig. 88 and fig. 25, p. 37)**. The flute of the gouge points in the direction of the cut,

Fig. 89
Rounding side from base

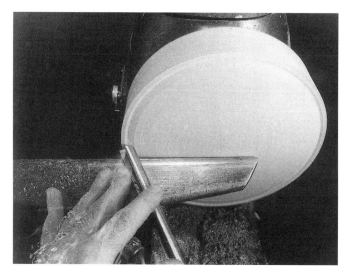

Fig. 90
Rounding side from base

Fig. 91
Cutting towards top of side

Fig. 92
Cutting towards top of side, close up

Fig. 93
Side of bowl, ground-back gouge

i.e. away from the work, and the part of the edge that does the cutting is the part between the centre of the flute and the bottom end of the edge. Before you start the lathe, work out the angle required to enable the edge to be supported by the bevel. When you start up the lathe you will notice that the edges of the work are blurred because it is not perfectly circular. As in all roughing-out cuts, you have to aim for the outermost edge.

If this were to be the outside of a bowl it is easier not to move the rest round to the side and true up the sides in a separate cut. If you are aiming to have a rounded profile, it is easier to do the sides of this shape starting from the base, which, because it is true, gives support to the bevel as you cut outwards to the side. **Figs. 89–90** show the first cuts in this process. Once you have rounded off the corner you can stop the lathe and move the rest around, so that when you do the top half of the side, the support is as close as possible to the work **(figs. 91–92)**. While making these cuts you have to be conscious of the shape you wish to make and the shape you are actually making. As an exercise you can copy the shape

of the bowl I am making in the photos. However, you will find bowl making a much more satisfying activity if you develop your own aesthetic preferences. Whatever shape you decide upon you will need to get into the habit of looking at the shape while you are turning, which necessitates wrenching your gaze from the tool tip and looking at the profile.

When you have a shape you can live with, you can smooth it with a scraper. Personally, I prefer to use the gouge with the bevel ground back **(see fig. 25, p. 37)**. Used as in **fig. 93**, cutting

Fig. 94
Side of bowl, ground-back gouge, smoothing cut

Fig. 95
Side of bowl, ground-back gouge, smoothing cut

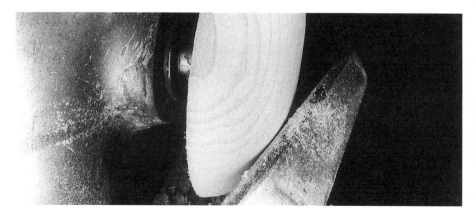

Fig. 96
Finish from 12.5mm ($\frac{1}{2}$in) gouge

just below the point, it removes wood quite quickly, but used as in (**figs. 94–95**), cutting with the side, it takes less off and produces a fine finish. Do be careful with this cut, however, because if you allow the tool to roll over too far the bevel will not support the edge and it will dig in.

If you can go over the whole of the outside of your shape in one flowing movement, you will find that you produce a smooth curve and finish as in **fig. 95**; but it is not easy and will come only with practice. If you examine the finish after this cut you will probably find that there are rough spots at two points on the outside where the end grain occurs. This is bound to be the case except in curly grained wood where the end grain will manifest itself more than twice! Experience alone will dictate the best way of getting rid of this roughness, but a method I frequently use before recourse to sanding is to apply cooking oil to the rough spots as in **fig. 97** and then doing a fine cut with the side of a 6.25mm ($\frac{1}{4}$in) ground-back gouge as in **fig. 98**. Because the tool has a thinner section it has a sharper edge and the oil makes the grain stand up which enables it to be cut more cleanly. **Fig. 99** shows the finish from this last cut.

It is better to practise these cuts until you nearly meet the screws that hold the blank, so that you have really mastered them before attempting to finish a piece. But after doing this several times you will probably be ready to go on to the next stage of reversing the blank so that you can practise hollowing out. If you elect to hold the blank on the lathe by means of screws and faceplate, you may well find it hard to centre the blank when you remount it, because the screws do not always go in exactly where you want them. What you need is some method of locating the faceplate precisely in the centre of the base. You can do this by mounting a disc of wood on the faceplate with either a spigot turned on it or a pin through it, and turning a recess or making a small hole in the base of the blank to locate in it. The screws can pass through the faceplate and disc and into the base. In fact, it is not always necessary to finish the whole of the outside of the bowl before remounting it. If you just finish off the base and roughly form the outside you should be able to remount the bowl on the faceplate. You then finish off the outside, correcting any assymetries caused by mis-aligning the faceplate before hollowing commences.

If, however, you do not mind having a recess in the base and intend to use an expanding chuck, you must first decide on the size of chuck inserts you will use. This will depend on the design of the bowl, but also on your level of skill. For your first efforts it is better to go for a larger base than may be aesthetically desirable, in the interests of safety.

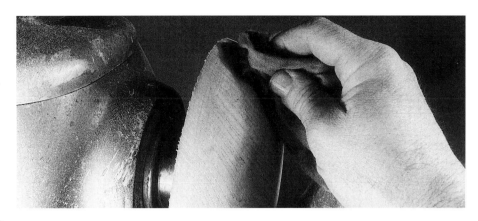

Fig. 97
Applying oil to rough spots

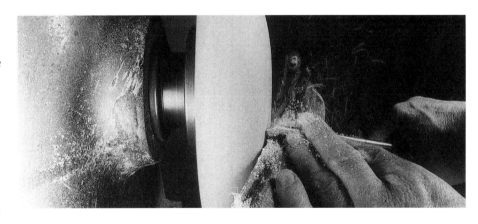

Fig. 98
Bowl gouge, 6.25mm ($\frac{1}{4}$in), finishing cut

Fig. 99
Finish from 6.25mm ($\frac{1}{4}$in) gouge

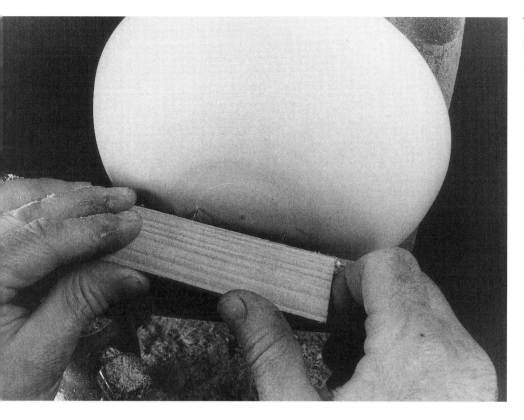

Fig. 100
Marking recess in base

With the tool techniques outlined above you will be able to make any sort of flatware, including breadboards, so I will now describe the making of bowls.

BOWL TURNING TECHNIQUES

A bowl can be a simple cylinder with its inside removed but that is not very aesthetically pleasing. A rounded profile looks nicer and if you get the curve of the sides and the size of the base just right it is very satisfying to look at. The size of the base is determined by practical as well as aesthetic considerations; a very small base can look very good but is not suitable for everyday use because it will not be very stable. First decide what purpose the item will serve and then design it accordingly. It would be easy if there were a mathematical formula to express the relation of the size of the base to any given size of bowl, but if there were it would be very boring. In the end, it all boils down to a matter of taste.

There is one design criterion which does seem to work and this is that you should make your shape a definite one. Consistent curves and distinct changes of direction convince the observer that the object was meant to be, and that is one of the secrets of giving an object 'presence'.

When you look at the side of a bowl your eye automatically follows the curve to its conclusion and, if this is buried deep under the surface it is standing on, the object has a heavy look. If, however, the curve seems to disappear just below the surface and then reappears up the other side the object looks lighter.

If you mount the bowl on a faceplate, the size of the base is restricted by the size of faceplate, which is not usually smaller than 75mm (3in). The same applies to expanding chucks, except that in their case you have to leave sufficient wood between the recess and the side of the bowl to stand up to the forces exerted by the chuck.

For a bowl 20cm (8in) wide a base 75mm (3in) wide should satisfy all aesthetic and practical criteria. If you use an expanding chuck the inserts will need to be 62.5mm (2½in).

You make the recess by first marking out its size with either a pair of compasses (only touch one point on the work while it is rotating otherwise it will catch) or a simple measuring device consisting of two nails in a piece of wood (fig. 100).

Hollow out the recess with a narrow gouge (fig. 101) and make the edge with a 12.5mm (½in) scraper (fig. 102). A scraper should be used with its edge lower than the rest so that if it digs in it does not impale itself too far. You will notice that the scraper I use (fig. 103) is specifically designed for the purpose: its edge is 10° less than a right angle so that it naturally produces a dovetail recess to fit the chuck.

When you are using such a chuck for the first time you should make the recess as deep as the inserts, but as your technique improves and catches become less frequent, you will find that you can get away with quite a shallow one. It is a good idea to check that the chuck fits the recess before you remove the blank from the faceplate.

The base should be finished off by sanding (see Chapter Ten). Do not attempt to sand the edge of

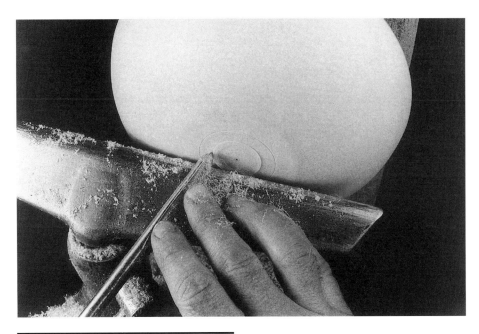

Fig. 101
Hollowing out recess with gouge

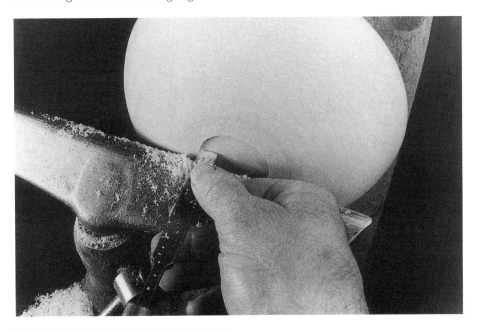

Fig. 102
Making edge of recess with scraper

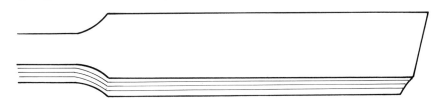

Fig. 103
Straight scraper 12.5mm (½in)

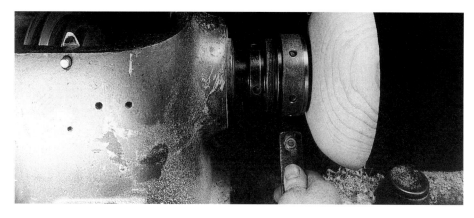

Fig. 104
Mounting blank on combination chuck

Fig. 105
Trueing up face of bowl

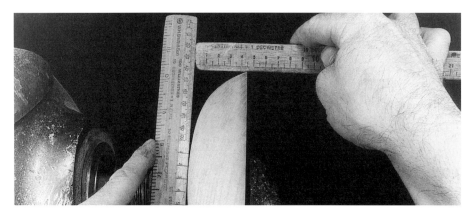

Fig. 106
Measuring depth of blank

the recess for the chuck as this will render it asymmetrical and will mean that the chuck will not fit.

When you mount the blank on the combination chuck on the inboard side of the lathe as in **(fig. 104)**, you will find it easier to tighten the chuck by holding the lathe spindle still with the spanner, so that you have one hand free to hold the bowl and the other to manipulate the spanner. This enables you to check the centricity of the bowl while tightening.

When the blank is tight and central you can true up the top face using the gouge you used to do the same job on the bottom **(fig. 105)**. You will need to find out how deep you can go before you reach the screws or the recess. It is best to leave at least 12mm ($\frac{1}{2}$in) in the bottom for strength and more if your screws intrude more than this.

To make sure that you do not go further than this, measure the depth of the blank **(fig. 106)** and subtract from that figure the thickness of the base. You will find it more comfortable to cut a funnel-shaped hole before drilling the depth hole as in **(fig. 107)** so that when the gouge is drilling the hole the hot steam can escape without burning your nail. Then hold the depth gouge **(see fig. 122, p. 95)** against a ruler and hold your thumb at the required depth as in **(fig. 108)**. Now you can push the gouge into the hole until your thumb reaches the top **(fig. 109)** and you will be able to see this hole as you deepen the bowl, and when it disappears, you know that you must go no further.

You will have already decided on the purpose of the bowl so that you can determine the thickness you are going to make the walls. A salad bowl needs walls thick enough to stand up to everyday use but an ornamental bowl can have walls as thin as you like. Do bear in mind that when anyone first sees an object and thinks about picking it up they unconsciously work out how heavy it is going to be. If they eventually pick it up and it is heavier or lighter than they think they will be surprised. If you do not want to surprise them and want to make a bowl that feels 'right', an even wall thickness is required. If you decide to make a thin bowl but the method of holding it predetermines that the base will be thick, it will not feel right. If your first attempts are held on by 18.75mm ($\frac{3}{4}$in) screws, that ought to be the eventual wall thickness. Even though it will look rather heavy at least it will feel right.

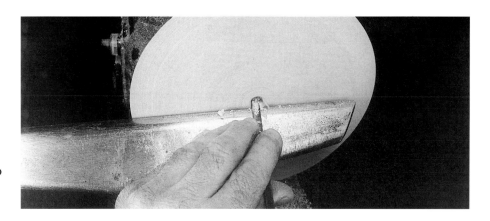

Fig. 107
Cutting opening to depth hole

Fig. 108
Marking depth gouge with depth

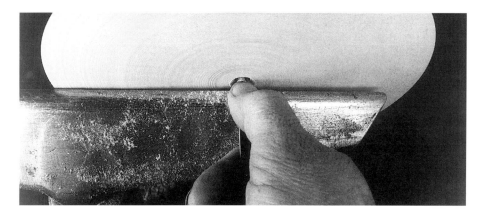

Fig. 109
Cutting depth hole

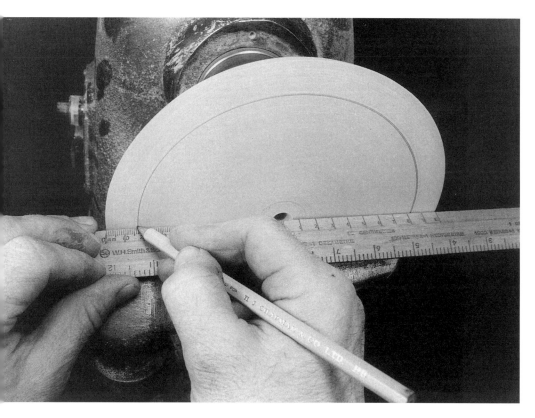

Fig. 110
Marking width of rim

A good, practical, wall thickness for a salad bowl of this size would be 9.37mm ($\frac{3}{8}$in). Mark the wall thickness on the top of the bowl with a pencil as in **fig. 110** but add a bit to take account of the possibility that you might make a mistake.

The initial hollowing is done with the 12.5mm ($\frac{1}{2}$in) gouge ground straight across **(see fig. 24, p. 37)**, in the same way as you flattened the base. However, on your first few bowls you may have a problem with producing a sharp shoulder where the top edge of the bowl meets the inside wall. This is because it is difficult to keep the bevel rubbing as you cut in around the sharp curve. You can solve this problem by forming the first few millimetres of hollowing at the top of the wall with the straight scraper **(fig. 111)**. This gives you something to rest the bevel of the gouge on and will prevent it from skating across the top **(fig. 112)**.

As you deepen the hollow, by roughly following the outside shape, you will have to raise the edge of the gouge by lowering the handle in order to keep the edge supported by the bevel **(fig. 113, overleaf)**. As you approach the centre you will have to lower the edge so that when you reach the middle the tool cuts right to it **(figs. 114–115)**. If you do not do this and you have not marked the depth with a hole, you will end up with a peak in the middle that can be difficult to remove. As you progress with the hollowing you must keep stopping the lathe to move the rest closer to the surface.

Figs. 116–118 overleaf show the last cuts as the bottom of the depth hole hoves into view. In the case of a deep bowl you will

Fig. 111
First cut with scraper

Fig. 112
First cut with gouge

Fig. 113
Raising tip of gouge as it goes in

Fig. 114
Lowering tip as it nears centre

Fig. 115
Tip level with centre at end of cut

Fig. 116
Last cut with straight gouge, start

Fig. 117
Last cut with straight gouge, halfway

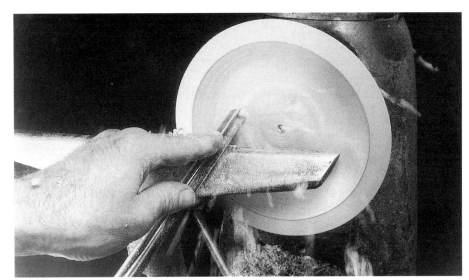

Fig. 118
Last cut with straight gouge, centre

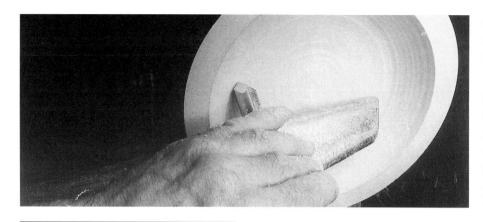

Fig. 119
Ground-back gouge in bowl

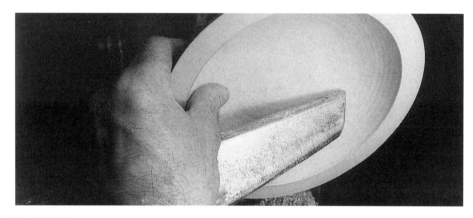

Fig. 120
Feeling wall thickness

Fig. 121
Finish from 12.5mm ($\frac{1}{2}$in) gouge

find that as you deepen the bowl it becomes difficult to keep the bevel in contact with the work. This is where the 12.5mm ($\frac{1}{2}$in) ground-back bevel gouge **(see fig. 25, p. 37)** is useful because the end has a tighter curve. Use this gouge to take out all of the rest of the inside **(fig. 119)** until you have an even wall thickness. This can be measured with callipers when the work is stationary but you should develop the capacity to gauge this by finger and thumb while the work is rotating **(figs. 119–120)**. Do be careful of the rim, however, which is sharp enough to cut deeply into flesh.

Fig. 121 shows the finish achieved with the 12.5mm ($\frac{1}{2}$in) ground-back gouge. There are grooves that will have to go and this is done with the 6.25mm ($\frac{1}{4}$in) gouge **(figs. 123–124)**. As on the outside base you can cut outwards in the bottom without running foul of centrifugal force but you will have to do the sides going inwards **(fig. 124)**. Fig. 125 shows the improved finish achieved with this tool.

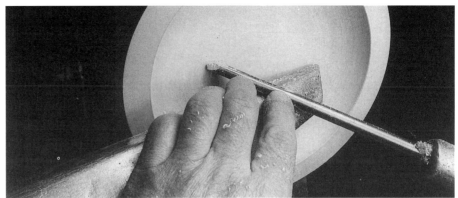

Fig. 123
Smoothing cut with 6.25mm ($\frac{1}{4}$in)
gouge, centre outwards

Fig. 124
Smoothing cut with 6.25mm ($\frac{1}{4}$in)
gouge, rim inwards

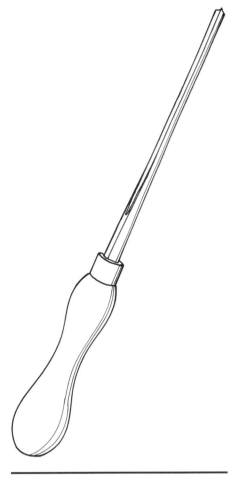

Fig. 122
Depth gouge 6.25mm ($\frac{1}{4}$in)

Fig. 125
Finish from 6.25mm ($\frac{1}{4}$in) gouge

Fig. 126
Smoothing with 37.5mm (1½in) scraper

Fig. 127
Finish from scraper

This finish can be further improved using the 37.5mm (1½in) half round scraper as in **fig. 126**. As with the scraper used for the recess in the base this tool should be used with the edge pointing down below the level of the rest which is positioned at, or slightly above, centre height. It is safer this way and you can achieve a

Fig. 128
Finished bowl

Fig. 129
Bottom of bowl showing ugly recess

smooth finish with a sharp tool
(**fig. 127**), but when you have
gained a lot more experience you
can try a smoothing cut with the
scraper pointing upwards. For
finishing techniques, see Chapter
Ten. **Fig. 128** shows the finished
bowl, and **fig. 129** shows the
ugly recess in the base which I
will remove by rechucking it.

In this chapter I have covered the hollowing of a bowl where the grain runs across the blank. This is the usual way the grain runs in a bowl, but there is no reason why you should not make a bowl with the grain running from the base to the top as in a goblet. In this case the gripping of the blank and the hollowing process are most efficiently carried out in quite different ways to that described above because of the way the grain is running. Screws do not grip well in end grain and if you hollow from the outside to the centre, you will be cutting the grain the wrong way. This is a more advanced technique, which I do not cover in this book.

–10

FINISHING

With practice you should gradually get to the stage where the finish from the tool needs less and less improvement. You will always find that there will be some rough patches that you cannot finish with the tool and the only answer to this will be sanding. Do not start sanding, however, before you are certain that you have finished with the tool, as abrasives leave small particles in the wood which can blunt edges.

Woodturners of the past are fondly recalled as needing no sandpaper, but I think the reasons for this have more to do with the rose-coloured spectacles with which we view them than any shortage of skill on the part of modern turners (who always use some). If they were loath to use abrasives it probably had more to do with the shortage of shark skin than anything else, and if they had had the range of abrasives available today they would probably be just as willing to use them as we are.

I am always highly suspicious of those who criticize a method on the basis that it was not used in the past. The one thing that professional turners of the past share with turners of the present is that they had to make a living – and did so by the most efficient means available.

I have already alluded to faults that can occur as a result of bad sanding. In fact, sanding can be done in such a way that you can avoid these; this requires a grasp of certain techniques which I shall elaborate.

ABRASIVES

Abrasives are described in terms of grit size (e.g. 60, 80, 100) which simply refers to the number of holes per unit area in the grid through which the abrasive particles pass. The lower the number, the larger the particle, i.e. the coarser it cuts. Abrasives are also described in terms of the weight of the paper if they are paper-backed.

The particles may be glass, garnet or aluminium oxide in order of increasing effectiveness, and may be bonded to paper or cloth. They can also be coated – which means that the particles have a covering of resin that tends to prevent the particles detaching themselves from the backing and also from getting clogged.

Glasspaper is not worth using because the grits detach too easily from the backing, and the grits themselves are not hard enough to stand up to the heat generated by the friction of the wood. Garnet paper is harder but the grits still tend to detach, particularly if the paper gets damp and also where the sheet is folded. Garnet has its uses but it is not meant for power sanding which is what you are doing when finishing on the lathe. Coated, cloth-backed aluminium oxide is more expensive than the other two but it lasts longer and produces a better finish – so that it is well worth the extra money.

The technique of using abrasives is to start with a grade that gets rid of the rough spots left by the tool, and to work up through a succession of grades that get rid of the grooves left by the previous grade. You should not start with a grade coarser than 80 grit because it will alter the shape left by the tool and you

Fig. 130
Sanding, 180 grit, straight section

Fig. 131
Sanding, 180 grit, cove

Fig. 132
Sanding inside

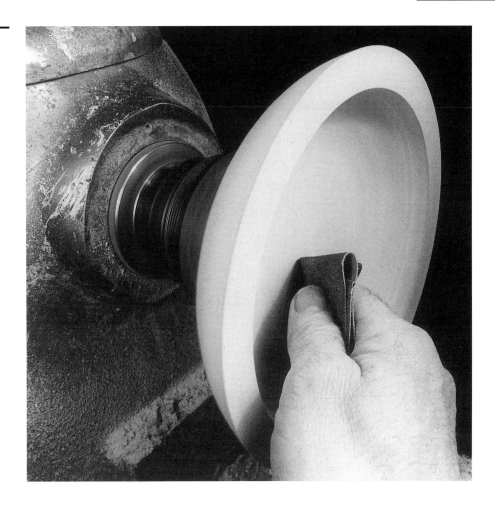

then work up through 100, 120, 180 and 220. I finish off with 0000 wire wool but do not use it on a wood such as oak, which corrodes steel, or on coarse woods which catch the wire fibres.

To avoid grooves getting too deep as you are sanding you should keep the abrasive moving across the surface. You should hold the abrasive so that if it catches in the work it can be pulled away from your hand. A good way to do this is to hold it under the work on top of the fingers with the palm facing upwards and gripped by the thumb. Be particularly careful in faceplate work as it is especially

easy to allow your hand to wander up accidentally over the centre, so that the direction of rotation is towards you – this can lead to broken fingers.

As you can see from **fig. 130**, where I am using 180 grit as my first grade on the cove and bead exercise, you can have your forefinger parallel with the axis of the work so that you get even pressure over a wide area on straight sections. In **fig. 131** my fingers are at right angles to the axis so that I am exerting even pressure over a curved surface. Use a piece of abrasive that is only as wide as you need so it is manoeuvrable, but do fold it three

times to protect your skin against the heat generated by friction. If you keep your abrasives in piles of the same grit size you will not waste time searching for the appropriate grade.

When I described flatware techniques I mentioned that difficult grain can be tamed with the application of a little oil or water (see pp. 68 and 97). This is even more useful in the case of bowls because of the presence of endgrain on at least two places on each surface. When you have obtained a surface that is as smooth as you can get from the tool you will need to sand it as in **fig. 132**, where I am using 100

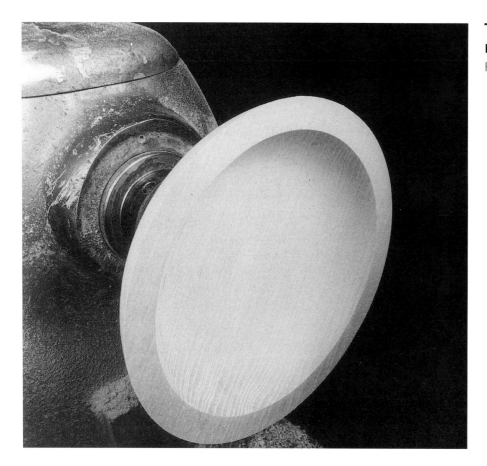

Fig. 133
Finish from 220 grit

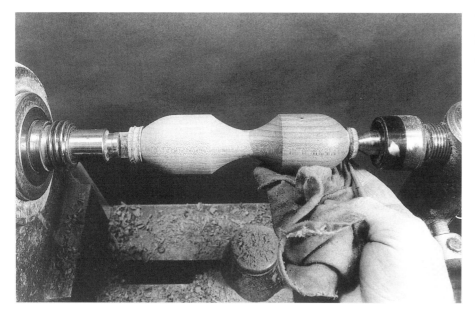

Fig. 134
Applying cooking oil

grit, which I followed up with 180 and then 220. **Fig. 133** shows the finish from 220 grit.

FINISHES

Once you have a smooth surface you can apply the finish of your choice. This will depend on the effect you want to achieve. If you are making an object that will be used with food then you should avoid a finish that is either poisonous or smelly. As a general rule finishes that sit on the surface and seal it, such as polyurethane, are a bad idea since wood moves and the finish ought to be able to move with it. I find that cooking oil is a good finish for kitchenware because it soaks into the wood and is easily reapplied as and when necessary. **Fig. 134** shows the application of cooking oil by cloth with the work stationary. You can see how it brings up the grain.

For small articles that need a shiny finish, such as lace bobbins, there are shellac-based finishes on the market which can be applied when the work is rotating. This is not suitable for larger objects because it is difficult to prevent the shellac from building up in rings which then have to be removed with abrasives.

For larger objects that will not be used with food I use Danish oil, which I apply with a cloth or brush and dry by buffing it with another cloth while it is rotating. The more coats you apply the

Fig. 135
Applying beeswax

Fig. 136
Buffing with cloth

shinier it gets. But if you decide that it is too shiny you can cut it back with a fine abrasive.

Whatever finish you use you can improve the feel by applying a thin layer of beeswax. This is done by holding a piece of the wax against the work while it is rotating (**fig. 135**). Move it quickly over the area because if it is too thick it becomes opaque, then buff with a cloth (**fig. 136**).

Fig. 137
Finish

Fig. 138
After application of oil

Fig. 137 shows the finish. Fig. 138 shows how some vegetable oil and beeswax will bring up the grain on a turned bowl. The best sort of cloth to use is something like an old 'T' shirt because the repeated washing will have removed the flock which can transfer itself to the work and stick in the finish.

There are some safety considerations to bear in mind when using cloth. Firstly, when you are holding cloth against a rotating piece make sure that you are holding it in such a way that if it catches in the work or wraps itself around the driving centre it will be pulled out of your hand (fig. 136). In other words do not wrap it around your fingers. Loose threads have a particular tendency to be caught and if they should do so on a fine piece it will be broken. Secondly, cloths impregnated with finish such as Danish oil catch fire spontaneously so should be stored in airtight vessels.

There is endless scope for experimentation in finishing. You may decide that you like a gloss finish or a textured or coloured one: this is where personal taste and exploration can lead you down some creative avenues.

AFTERWORD

In Part Two I have described all the techniques you need to produce a wide range of spindle and faceplate turnings. I have not described methods for producing specific items because I believe that if you master the basics first, then you can go on to apply those skills to whatever project takes your fancy. The sort of items you can make with the spindle techniques include tool handles, a wide range of kitchen tools (such as rolling pins, steak bashers and honey dippers), ballusters and chair legs, and hence stools if you have some joining skills. With the faceplate techniques you can make salad bowls, breadboards, platters, cheeseboards and candle holders.

Because turning is a craft that enables you to change radically the shape of a piece of wood in a very short time, and because those of us who demonstrate the craft produce well-finished items comparatively quickly, there is a temptation for the beginner to think that their chosen craft is easily mastered. In fact, the only reason why professional turners are proficient is not that they are particularly gifted but simply that they are turning all the time. If they do not become efficient they do not earn enough to live on.

Just as any painter does not produce a great work of art as soon as they start, so I would ask you to exercise patience and learn to do the simple things well before attempting anything too ambitious. Practising skills has never been very popular, as I remember when I tried to learn the piano. The reason why I did not succeed was that I did not want it badly enough; a degree of obsession and bloody-minded persistance was what it took for me to learn to turn.

My next two books will describe more advanced techniques in spindle and faceplate work and if you add these to the skills learnt by practising the methods detailed in this book you should be able to turn your hand to anything.

USEFUL ADDRESSES

WOODTURNING ASSOCIATIONS

Association of Woodturners of
  Great Britain
Hon Sec Hugh O'Neill
5 Kent Gardens
Eastcote
Ruislip
Middlesex HA4 8RX
England

American Association of
  Woodturners
Administrator Mary Redig
667 Harriet Avenue
Shoreview
MN 55126
USA

Canadian Woodturners
  Association
Box 8812
Ottawa
Ontario KIG 3JI
Canada

Association of Pole Lathe Turners
Hon Sec Hugh Robert
Carreg Rhys
Paradwys
Bodogan
Anglesey LL62 5PB
Wales

EQUIPMENT SUPPLIERS

Lathes

LRE Machinery & Equipment Co
Bramco House
Turton Street
Golborne
Warrington WA3 3AB
England

Craft Supplies Ltd
The Mill
Miller's Dale
Buxton
Derbyshire SK17 8SN
England

Craft Supplies WA
1287 East 1120 South
Provo
UT 84606
USA

Axminster Power Tool Centre
Chard Street
Axminster
Devon EX13 5DZ
England

For plans of a pole lathe:

High Wycombe Museum
Castle Hill
High Wycombe
England

Dust Extractors

Air Plants (Sales) Ltd
295 Aylestone Rd
Leicester LE2 7PB
England

P&J Dust Extraction Ltd
Lordwood Industrial Estate
Chatham
Kent ME5 8PF
England

Airstream Dust Helmets
16 Division St W
Elbow Lake
MN 56531
USA

Craft Supplies and Craft Supplies
USA as above

Axminster Power Tools as above

Tools

Henry Taylor (Tools) Ltd
The Forge
Lowther Road
Sheffield S6 2DR
England

Robert Sorby Ltd
Greenland Rd
Sheffield S9 5EW
England

Gerry Glaser
Glaser Engineering Co. Inc.
P.O. Box 2417
Newport Beach
CA 92663
USA

Timber Suppliers

Milland Fine Timber Ltd
Rakers Yard
Liphook
Hants GU30 7JS
England

Ecological Trading Co
London Eco Timbers Ltd
Unit 5
Gibson Business Centre
800 High Road
Tottenham
London N17 0DH
England

Tiverton Sawmills
Harsdon Sawmills
Blundell's Road
Tiverton
Devon EX16 4DE
England

Colin Baker
Crown Hill
Halberton
Devon EX16 7AY
England

RECOMMENDED READING

MAGAZINES

Woodturning & Woodworking Today
Castle Place
166 High Street
Lewes
East Sussex BN7 1XU
England

Fine Woodworking
PO Box 5506
Newtown
CT 06470
USA

Woodworker
Argus Specialist Publications
Argus House
Boundary Way
Hemel Hempstead
Herts HP2 7ST
England

Practical Woodworking
IPC Magazines
Kings Reach Tower
Stamford Street
London SE1 9LS
England

Good Woodworking
30 Monmouth Street
Bath
Avon BA1 2BW
England

American Woodworking
33 E Minor Street
Emmaus
PA 18098
WA

BOOKS

Hand or Simple Turning: Principles and Practice, Holtzapffel's Turning and Mechanical Manipulation Vol 4, John Jacob Holtzapffel, Dover New York (Constable UK), 1991

Woodturning and Design, Ray Key, B.T. Batsford Ltd, London, 1985

The Woodturner's Workbook, Ray Key, B.T. Batsford Ltd, London, 1992

Creative Woodturning, Dale Nish, Stobart & Son Ltd, London (Brighane University Press, WA), 1978

Woodturning, Klaus Pracht, B.T. Batsford Ltd, London (Rudolf Muller, Germany), 1991

Turning Wood, Richard Raffan, The Taunton Press, 1985

Turned Bowl Design, Richard Raffan, The Taunton Press, 1987

Shapes for Woodturners, David Weldon, B.T. Batsford Ltd, London, 1992

The Anatomy of Wood: its Diversity and Variability, K Wilson and DJB White, Stobart & Son Ltd London, 1986

Woodturning, W.J. Wooldridge. B.T. Batsford Ltd, London, 1991

INDEX